ISTANBUL

in your pocket

MICHELIN

Main Contributor: A J Byfield

Photograph Credits
All photos supplied by The Travel Library
A Amsel title page, 103, 115; Alan Bedding 54, 57, 78, 80, 100, 104, 106; Stuart Black front cover, 5, 9, 10, 11, 12 (left, right), 14, 17, 18, 21, 23, 28, 29, 31, 33, 34, 35, 37, 39, 40, 42, 44, 45, 47, 48, 49, 50, 51, 58, 59, 60, 61, 62, 63, 64, 65, 67, 68, 70, 71, 72, 73, 74, 75, 76, 79, 83, 93, 98, 102, 105, 109; James Davis Travel Photography 87; Iain Fairweather 25, 26, 85; David Forman 6, 90; Oldrich Karasek back cover, 88, 113; Andre Laubier 89; Grant Pritchard 53, 94, 97, 117, 120; Simon Reddy 41; R Richardson 110; Gino Russo 20.

Front cover: Blue Mosque at sunset; back cover: ferry boat on the Bosphorus; title page: fish market

MANUFACTURE FRANÇAISE DES PNEUMATIQUES MICHELIN

Place des Carmes-Déchaux – 63000 Clermont-Ferrand (France)

© Michelin et Cie. Propriétaires-Éditeurs 1997

Dépôt légal Mai 97 – ISBN 2-06-651501-9 – ISSN 1272-1689

No part of this publication may be reproduced in any form

without the prior permission of the publisher.

Printed in Spain 10-98/2

MICHELIN TYRE PLC
Tourism Department
The Edward Hyde Building
38 Clarendon Road
WATFORD Herts WD1 1SX - UK
☎ (01923) 415000

MICHELIN TRAVEL PUBLICATIONS
Editorial Department
One Parkway South
GREENVILLE, SC 29615
☎ 1-800 423-0485

CONTENTS

INTRODUCTION

Byzantium…Constantinople…İstanbul: the
Queen of Cities and capital of, it could be
said, two of the most enduring empires the
world has ever seen, with an event-filled
history dating back 26 centuries. The
Byzantine and Ottoman empires were not
only politically and militarily mighty, they
were also highly cultured, and their art and
architecture uniquely innovative. With a
pedigree such as this, the city today can be
thought of as an open-air museum
celebrating Roman, Byzantine and Ottoman
prowess and extravagance. It remains a city
of superlatives. Its protective land walls are
the most formidable ever built. The 6C
Haghia Sophia (Ayasofya) remained the
largest church in Christendom for 700 years.
Its surviving late Byzantine mosaics are the
most exquisite to be found anywhere. And
even its latter-day rugs and chandeliers rank
among the largest in the world. Yet İstanbul
is much more than just an exceptional
collection of buildings and fine furnishings
from bygone times. Today, it remains the
spiritual and industrial capital of the
Republic of Turkey (Ankara is now the
political capital). And its swelling population
includes a rich blend of ethnic minorities,
including Armenians, Greeks, Poles and Jews.

At times it is noisy, overcrowded and
polluted. So do not expect staid parks and
spotless sidewalks, although these are
becoming more frequent. Instead, be
adventurous, and let yourself go with the
flow. You are sure to be captivated.

*A bustling open-air market, with the Galata
Tower in the background.*

GEOGRAPHY

The Byzantine chronicler Procopius wrote of Constantinople in the 6C AD, that 'The sea forms a garland about the city.' It is these waters – the Bosphorus, Golden Horn and the Sea of Marmara – which lend to the city so much of its character and charm. Yet it is these same waters that confuse so many first-time visitors, unsure as to whether they are looking at the straits or the Horn or, indeed, whether they are standing in Europe or Asia.

Were any city to have a perfect 'text book' location, İstanbul would have it. The old city sits along a narrow finger of land, circled on three sides by the sea, and with an easily-defended landward exposure to the west. To the north, it is bounded by the Golden Horn, one of the world's finest natural harbours, in which a complete naval fleet could seek shelter. Situated on shipping routes between the Black Sea and the Mediterranean, and on land routes between

View from the Galata Tower looking south-east across the Golden Horn and Topkapı Palace with the Sea of Marmara and Princes' Islands beyond.

Europe and Asia, the city occupies one of the world's most strategic sites.

To familiarise yourself with the city and its layout, it is worth climbing the 14C Galata Tower (by lift) and taking in the stupendous view from its balcony, some 60m (197ft) high. First locate the **Bosphorus Bridge**, the world's fourth-largest suspension bridge at the time of its completion. This straddles **the Bosphorus**, the incomparably beautiful straits that link the **Black Sea** in the north to the **Sea of Marmara** in the south, and separate Europe from Asia. Everything on the far shore of the straits lies in Asian Turkey (more commonly called Anatolia, representing about 97 per cent of the Turkish land surface). The hill to the right of the suspension bridge is **Büyük Çamlıca** (the Hill with Pines), and with its rash of radio masts, it provides a useful landmark to get your bearings. Further around, but still firmly on Asian soil, are the ancient settlements of **Üsküdar** and **Kadıköy**. It was in the latter that the first wave of Greeks settled, naming their new settlement Chalcedon. Whilst not blessed with the same wealth of monuments as the European half of the city, both Üsküdar and Kadıköy are, nevertheless, of considerable historic interest.

Beyond these settlements, the Bosphorus widens, merging with the Sea of Marmara. In the distance, beyond the mouth of the Bosphorus, lie the **Princes' Islands**, an archipelago of nine islands noted for their fine wooden mansions, and above all, peace and quiet.

Turning to the European side of the city, the **Golden Horn** can be seen, striking off to the right of the Bosphorus, and crossed by a

series of smaller road bridges. Immediately below the tower is the **Galata Bridge**, and beyond this the oldest part of the city, with its magical skyline of minarets, commendably free of tower blocks. The old sector of the city is a finger-like projection of land, surrounded by water on its north, east and south sides. At the extremity of this 'finger' is Saray Burnu, where King Byzas constructed the city's first acropolis 'opposite the land of the blind', and where today stand the pavilions and gardens of the **Topkapı Palace**, for nearly 400 years home to the most powerful sultans of the Ottoman Empire.

To the right of the palace building stands the formidable bulk of **Ayasofya**, Emperor Justinian's legendary Byzantine church, built 1 400 years ago, and which remained for 700 years the largest religious building in Christendom. Nearby is the equally imposing **Blue Mosque**, most popular of the city's imperial Ottoman mosques, with its elegantly proportioned exterior and six slender minarets. Formerly, this general area was the heart of the Byzantine city.

The old city spreads beyond, with its numerous mosques and churches. Though masked by buildings, it boasts seven hills, like Rome, most crowned by fine mosque complexes. The First Hill overlooks the confluence of the Bosphorus and the Sea of Marmara and is surmounted by the Topkapı Palace. The Seventh Hill lies in the far distance, close to the **Theodosian Land Walls**, perhaps the most unassailable walls ever built, and which mark the boundary of the old city. Looking up the Golden Horn, past the Imperial Docks, it is possible to see the high, arching bridge of the E 5 circular

motorway, which links with the first Bosphorus Bridge. This route more or less runs parallel to the Land Walls. Beyond the motorway bridge lies **Eyüp**, one of the most venerated shrines in the Muslim world, for here lies Prophet Mohammed's loyal standard bearer, Eyüp Ensari.

Note the 'European' architectural style of the district of **Pera**, lying around the base of the tower. As the city became increasingly Westernised during the second half of the 19C, so bankers and business men developed this district, which today bears the name **Beyoğlu**. But the city is still changing: in the distance, looking north, lie the sparkling new office blocks and shopping malls that form İstanbul's current business district, testament to Turkey's current period of rapid industrial growth.

View south from Galata Tower showing the Galata Bridge in the foreground, and Ayasofya on the skyline to the left with the Blue Mosque just to its right. The Mosque of Süleyman the Magnificent is on the far right.

HISTORY

İstanbul's superb situation, easily defended and straddling main shipping and land trade routes between east and west, was recognised perhaps as early as the 8C BC. Through the city's long and tumultuous history, Arabs, Avars, Bulgars, Byzantines, Goths, Huns, Lombards, Ottomans, Persians, Romans, Slavs and Turks have all sought to control this strategic position.

The Birth of Byzantium

The city was founded around the late 8C to the early 7C BC as a Greek colony by the **Megarians**, seeking to evade continuing assaults by the Dorians on the Greek mainland. The first wave of settlers founded **Chalcedon**, situated on the Asian side of the Bosphorus near modern-day Kadıköy. The second wave – led by Byzas – took the wise precaution of consulting the Delphic oracle before setting out, and were advised to colonise the lands opposite Chalcedon. Byzas chose to settle on the superbly defensible hill of Saray Burnu – where the Topkapı Palace stands today – and founded a settlement which he named after himself, **Byzantium**. He concluded that the earlier settlers of Chalcedon must have been 'blinded' (hence the name 'the Land of the Blind') to have foregone the opportunities offered by his European location.

By this time, Greece had developed important trade links with settlements on the fertile shores of the Black Sea. Byzantium accordingly developed rapidly as a staging post, becoming prosperous from the custom fees levied on merchant shipping passing through the Bosphorus.

Hittite figures in the Museum of the Ancient Orient.

Head of Alexander the Great in the Archaeological Museum.

Peace reigned for about 150 years, but the city's increasing prosperity attracted unwelcome attention. Byzantium was in turn pawn to the Spartans, and later surrendered without a struggle to **Alexander the Great**. But the death of Alexander saw the start of the gradual decline of Greece as the principal power in the region.

In 133 BC, Byzantium bequeathed all its powers to Rome in exchange for retaining its freedom. As a result, it largely enjoyed peace – under the umbrella of *Pax Romana* – until the closing years of the 2C AD. Peace evaporated when two rival emperors, **Septimius Severus** and **Pescennius Niger**, brought about civil war. The Byzantines sided with the latter, but on his defeat in AD 196 the victorious Septimius Severus put the city under siege, tearing down the Megarian Walls and burning the city to the ground. In recognition of the city's strategic importance he soon set to rebuilding Byzantium. New walls were erected, enclosing an area approximately twice that of the original settlement. The steady expansion of the city had thus begun.

New Rome – Constantine's City

In the early years of the 4C, under the **Emperor Diocletian**, the Roman Empire was split into two sections, west and east, each ruled by an emperor, supported by a caesar. Diocletian chose to rule as emperor of the Eastern Empire from his capital at Nicomedia, modern-day İzmit. Following Diocletian's reign, **Licinius** and **Constantine** fought for control of the whole empire. Constantine eventually defeated his rival, and after a brief spell in Rome, ultimately chose Byzantium as the new capital of the Roman Empire. The Emperor himself

The Valens Aqueduct was part of a complex water-supply network created by the Romans (see p.60).

marked out the boundary of new defensive walls, and began his programme of transforming Byzantium into the most magnificent of cities. Constantine dedicated his city to the Holy Trinity and the Mother of God. It was to be called 'New Rome', but the name never stuck. Instead, it became known as **Constantinople**, Constantine's city.

Rise of the Byzantines

The defence of the city was paramount. First sea walls were constructed along the shores of the Sea of Marmara (2C) and along the Golden Horn (from AD 438). Then during the first half of the 5C, the formidable land walls were built by Theodosius II, in an arc stretching for nearly 7km (4.3 miles) from the Golden Horn to the Sea of Marmara thus completing the circle of defence. With the strategic safety of the city resolved, the Byzantines could turn their attentions to other important matters, most notably religion. Constantine had welcomed **Christianity** to the city in the 4C, but Christians remained a minority amongst the city's largely pagan population. It took until the early 6C for Constantinople to become predominately Christian. A series of ecumenical councils were assembled with the aim of establishing a standard orthodox religious doctrine for the Church. This was of considerable importance, for seemingly the city's whole population took a personal interest in addressing these issues; rioting often followed if matters were not resolved satisfactorily. By far the most serious dispute followed Emperor Leo III's declaration against the display and veneration of figurative icons in homes and churches. In 730, he banned their display and ordered

A mosaic showing two children being led on the back of a camel. This mosaic, now in the Mosaic Museum (see p.45), is from the remains of the Great Palace of the Byzantine emperors and probably dates from around AD 500.

their destruction, including frescoes and mosaics in churches. The empire was split into two factions: the Iconodules, supporters of icon veneration, and the Iconoclasts, those who agreed with the views of Leo. Violent disputes followed, and not until 843 was the dispute finally resolved. As a result of the **Iconoclastic Crisis**, very few works of figurative Byzantine art predating the dispute survive.

Like Constantine, other powerful emperors adorned the city with fine religious buildings. The most prolific builder of all was **Emperor Justinian the Great**, who rebuilt the city with a vengeance after the highly destructive Nika Riots of 532. Five years later, Constantinople was the greatest city on earth, its crowning glory Ayasofya (Haghia Sophia or the Church of the Divine Wisdom), which was to so greatly influence the works of later Ottoman architects.

A mosaic from Ayasofya depicting Emperor Justinian (on the left) offering the church to the Blessed Virgin and the infant Jesus. On the right Emperor Constantine the Great offers a model of Constantinople.

An Empire in Decline

The history of the Byzantine Empire is one of endless expansion and contraction. Under emperors such as Heraclius, and generals such as Belisarius, the Empire expanded vastly, often to collapse only decades later under the rule of more feeble-minded successors. At its height, during the reign of **Emperor Heraclius** (610-641), the Empire extended around the Mediterranean and stretched as far as Armenia and Roman Mesopotamia. However, by the 11C the Byzantine Empire went into steady decline. A long succession of weak and ineffectual rulers failed to resolve serious internal troubles of the Empire, or to combat the external threats posed by new and stronger enemies appearing around its borders. On a number of occasions, the enemy came perilously close to the city itself, usually to be deflected by the city's defensive walls. However, invading forces twice penetrated the defences successfully.

The city was first overrun by the mercenaries of the **Fourth Crusade**, motivated both by greed and a desire for vengeance for the thousands of Venetians slain by the Byzantines a few decades earlier. On 13 April 1204, led by Enrico Dandolo, Doge of Venice, the sea walls were breached and the Crusaders poured into the city, stripping it of its wealth and destroying what remained in an orgy of drunken destruction. Despite their professed Christianity, no building was spared by the looters, not even Justinian's great church of Ayasofya. Perhaps in a moment of imprudence, Dandalo, the man who was responsible above all others for the

15

destruction of the city, chose to be buried in the sanctuary of Ayasofya. When the Latins were finally expelled by the Greek Emperor Michael VIII Palaeologus in 1261, Dandalo's bones were thrown unceremoniously to the street dogs.

Although the city had been won back, the Byzantine Empire had been gradually disintegrating for years, under repeated attack on many fronts. As far back as 1071, in distant Asia Minor, the Byzantines suffered a humiliating defeat by the Selçuk Turks at the **Battle of Manzikert**, allowing the Turks to spread unopposed across the whole of modern-day Anatolia, as far as the Sea of Marmara. With them came hordes of nomadic Turkoman tribesmen, who carved up the former Byzantine territory into a series of principalities, each governed by a warlord. The Turks, who moved into Bithynia to the south of the Sea of Marmara, were followers of **Ertuğrul**. It was his son, **Osman**, who founded (around 1288) a principality which was to expand into the Osmanlı (Ottoman) Empire.

The Ottoman Empire

By 1452, the Ottomans had largely encircled the city, under the command of **Sultan Mehmet II**. So weakened were the Byzantines by this stage, that Mehmet forced them to relinquish land along the Bosphorus, on which he built the formidable fortress of Rumeli Hisarı. With its completion, in just four months, essential Byzantine supply routes to the fertile Black Sea shores were severed. With naval forces stationed in the Sea of Marmara, Mehmet began his final onslaught on the city in April 1453.

Mehmet's land forces amassed outside the land walls and pounded the walls with giant cannons. The Byzantines barred access into the Golden Horn by means of a giant chain, but Mehmet overcame this in a display of military genius: part of the Ottoman fleet was pulled on rollers over the ridge near Galata. Outnumbered by ten to one, and surrounded on all sides, the Byzantines were finally overwhelmed.

Seven weeks after the beginning of the siege, on 29 May 1453, the Ottomans broke into city: within hours the Byzantines gave up all resistance. Mehmet himself rode to Ayasofya, and ordered its conversion to a mosque. The Conqueror began a programme of building; new palaces were built (replacing the Great Palace of the Byzantine emperors), and the Mosque of Mehmet the Conqueror (Fatih Mehmet Camii) was constructed. However, other religions were not expelled: both the Conqueror and his successor, Sultan Beyazit II, actively encouraged Armenians, Greeks

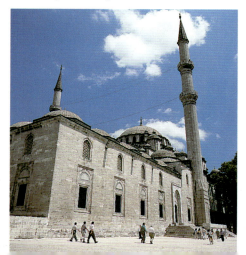

The Mosque of Mehmet the Conqueror was started just ten years after the Ottoman conquest of the city. Most of the original building was destroyed in an earthquake in 1766.

and Jews to settle in an attempt to inject life into the city's economy.

Like the Byzantine Empire, the Ottoman Empire followed the same pattern of expansion and contraction before its final demise. Great leaders such as **Sultan Süleyman the Magnificent** created an all-powerful empire that encompassed an area even greater than that of the Byzantines. Military successes generated abundant revenue, so Süleyman's reign (1520-1566) saw a renaissance in art and architecture. Under the expert eye of the most celebrated of all Ottoman architects, **Sinan**, the city was graced by some of the most magnificent mosque complexes ever constructed.

The Mosque of Sultan Süleyman the Magnificent still commands a view over the Golden Horn.

The Sick Man of Europe

Yet in just over a century after the death of Süleyman, the empire started to show signs of decay. In 1683, the Ottomans failed, for the second time, to take Vienna, and from this point onwards its territories started to shrink. More often than not, the reigning sultans preferred to spend their hours in the harem, rather than on the battlefield: corruption, intrigue and debauchery were very much the order of the day. By the end of the 18C remedial action was urgently required, and the empire looked to the west for solutions. **Sultan Selim III** (1789-1807) and his immediate successors undertook to introduce reforms, seeking to reorganise the Ottoman army and other institutions along western lines. By 1876, an Ottoman Constitution was in place, and its first parliament convened the following year. But these actions came too late to save the empire, which by now was more commonly referred to as the 'Sick Man of Europe'. By the end of the 19C, Bulgaria, Greece, Montenegro, Romania and Serbia had become independent states, free from Turkish domination. In 1912, during the **First Balkan War**, the empire lost virtually all its remaining European territories to the Greeks, Bulgars and Serbs.

The internal politics within the empire were in chaos, too. On his accession to the throne in 1876, **Sultan Abdül Hamit II** revoked the constitution and dissolved parliament. It had operated for just a year. He, in turn, was deposed by the 'Young Turks' movement in 1909 under the leadership of **Enver Paşa**, who established a military dictatorship in his place, relegating the sultan to the role of mere puppet.

Birth of a Republic

Enver Paşa was to make a fatal mistake in 1914 when he allied the empire with the Germans and the Central Powers, against Britain and her Allies, during the **First World War**. With the defeat of the Central Powers, the Allies set out to carve up the remaining fragments of the empire amongst themselves. On 15 May 1919, a Greek force landed in Smyrna (modern-day İzmir) and began advancing into western Asia Minor. Furthermore, the reigning **Sultan Mehmet VI**, a puppet of the Allies in occupied İstanbul, was forced into signing the **Treaty of Sevres**, by which the Ottoman Empire retained control over İstanbul and small parts of Asia Minor, whilst accepting the loss of lands already controlled by the Allied forces. For the Turks this was the last straw. Under the leadership of **Mustafa Kemal** – later **Atatürk** – the Turks were galvanised into action. In 1919, Atatürk rallied his people in Sivas, and called upon them to fight their own war of national independence. The following year he presided over the establishment of a new Turkish National Assembly, which formed a government in direct opposition to the sultan. The **Turkish War of Independence** began in 1919, and by September 1922 the Greek army was forced to withdraw from Anatolia. By November 1922, the Turkish National Assembly declared the Ottoman sultanate obsolete; in July 1923, the Treaty of Versailles was signed, establishing the

A bust of Atatürk framed by the Turkish flag.

boundaries of modern Turkey; and on 29 October 1923, the National Assembly proclaimed the founding of the **Republic of Turkey**. Atatürk, who had risen from minor general to national hero, became the Republic's first president.

ARCHITECTURE AND ART

Some of the finest 14C Iconoclastic mosaics, such as this depicting the death of the Virgin Mary, are to be found in Kariye Camii (St Saviour in Chora).

There is no better place to learn about Byzantine and Ottoman architecture than İstanbul and its surrounding towns of Bursa, Edirne and İznik. Central to the way of life in both the Christian and Islamic city were the religious buildings, many of which have survived.

The **classical Byzantine church** took the form of a *basilica*, a rectangular space with a

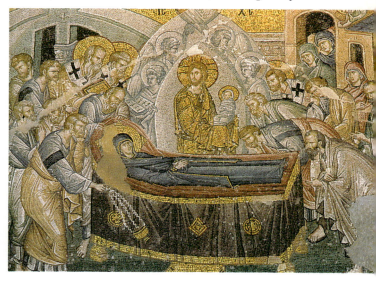

large central nave, bordered by two side aisles. At its eastern end a projecting semi-circular *apse* housed the altar, whilst at the opposite end, one or two corridors (the *narthex* and *exonarthex*) separated the entrance from the nave. This design developed from the earliest basilicas which had simple pitched roofs (such as İmrahor Camii). Later, domed roofs were introduced as, for example, by Justinian at Aya İrini and Ayasofya. Later styles diversified to include churches with circular or polygonal central naves (as at Küçük Ayasofya), or with cross-domes. In most cases, Byzantine churches were made of bricks and mortar.

The earlier churches were decorated inside with fine marble panelling, and gold mosaic, but later figurative mosaics became the norm. None of the pictorial examples predating the 9C survive, victims of the Iconoclastic Crisis. Fortunately, the end of Iconoclasm saw the creation of fine new mosaics; those in Ayasofya date from the 9C-12C, but undoubtedly the finest are to be found in Kariye Camii (St Saviour in Chora), dating from the time of the last renaissance in Byzantine art, during the 14C.

Ottoman architects looked to Ayasofya for inspiration, and sought to match or better it in magnificence. However, many of the earliest **mosques** were simple, comprising small rectangular rooms covered by a plain pitched roof or dome. From this basic structure, two styles evolved. The first was the **multi-domed (Ulu Cami) style**, in which the area available to worshippers could be vastly increased by supporting many small domes on a forest of columns. This was, however, considered too cluttered by many architects. The second style was the **double**

The magnificent domed interior of the Mosque of Sultan Süleyman the Magnificent.

(Bursa) style, in which the domed prayer hall was preceded by a second equally-sized domed hall, housing the ablution fountain.

It was from this second type that the great **classical mosques** evolved (1500-1650). In time, the second (ablution) hall developed into an open inner courtyard (first seen in the Üç Şerefeli Camii, Edirne). Further, with growing experience and expertise, as the main prayer halls increased vastly in size, the sense of space was often greatly increased by the addition of two or more semi-domes. Ultimately, these classical mosques, such as the Süleymaniye Camii, İstanbul, and the Selimiye Camii, Edirne, came to rival Ayasofya in size and majesty.

In the classical mosques, decoration took two principal forms: rich arabesque painting (of which little remains), and tile panelling, typically from the kilns of İznik. The southeast wall of each mosque contains the *mihrab*, the niche indicating the direction of Mecca to worshippers. To its right is the *minber*, the elevated pulpit from which the imam preaches his Friday sermon.

The larger mosques formed the centrepiece to the Ottoman *külliye*, or mosque complex, which often included a public baths (*hamam*), primary school, college (*medrese*), public kitchen (*imaret*), library, hospital and other institutions. These were either provided free of charge to the public, or were used to generate income for the upkeep of the mosque.

THE PEOPLE AND CULTURE

İstanbul is a multicultural, cosmopolitan city. Whilst the majority of the population claim Ottoman Turkish ancestry, there are substantial minorities such as Albanians, Armenians, Greeks, Jews, Kurds and Poles. An increasing proportion of the city's inhabitants are from the rural heartland of Anatolia attracted by the city and in search of a better life. Only in the last few years has the majority of the Turkish population become urban, and this trend seems set to continue. The result is a continual migration of up to 500 000 people from villages into the city every year. The city's current population is estimated at between 10 and 15 million, but the precise figure is not known.

Modern-day crowds at Beyazit Square.

The settlers often live in the seemingly endless sprawling suburbs, including the famous *gecekondu* shanty towns, in which the houses are built overnight to avoid the need for planning permission. Needless to say, such a strongly rural population is highly conservative, and most are devout Muslims.

Today, İstanbul is a city of extraordinary extremes. On the streets, the numbers of Mercedes and BMWs must be one of the highest of any European city, reflecting İstanbul's recent successes as the business capital of Turkey. Cheek-by-jowl are the families that have recently moved to the city from the countryside; with a greater range of jobs available, most would accept that life has improved after their move (albeit often measured simply in terms of televisions and washing machines). If all the peoples of İstanbul have one thing in common, it is their common desire to make the most of life.

MUST SEE

For the first-time visitor to İstanbul, there is a wealth of places to visit, but the following ten sights should not be missed.

Ayasofya★★★ (Haghia Sophia, The Church of the Divine Wisdom)

Justinian's great church dominates the skyline of the old city and remained the largest church in Christendom for 700 years, inspiring awe and wonderment among medieval and modern travellers alike.

Topkapı Sarayı★★★ (Topkapı Palace)

This amazingly complex palace houses an unbelievable hoard of riches – testament to the overwhelming power of the Ottoman Empire at its peak.

Sultan Ahmet Camii★★★
(Blue Mosque)

This is the best-loved of all the city's great mosques, with its six minarets and vast panels of blue tiles inside.

Kapalı Çarşı★★★
(Grand Bazaar)

Lose yourself amongst the 4 000 shops and search for oriental bargains: old copperware, Turkish carpets and kilims and even belly-dancing costumes from *One Thousand and One Nights.*

Archaeological Museums Complex★★★

A complex of three museums tracing the history of man's occupation of Anatolia from earliest times, and

The rich delights of the Grand Bazaar.

displaying the Code of Hammurabi (the law inscribed on clay tablets from ancient Babylon), examples of jewellery from Troy, and exquisite sarcophagi from Sidon.

Kariye Camii★★★
(Church of St Saviour in Chora)
Enter this small Byzantine church and marvel at exquisite mosaics and frescoes, regarded by many as the finest in existence.

Süleymaniye Camii★★★
(Mosque of Sultan Süleyman the Magnificent)
The most magnificent mosque complex in the city, built by the most talented Ottoman architect for the all-powerful Sultan Süleyman the Magnificent.

Yerebatan Sarayı★★ (Basilica Cistern)
This cool and tranquil Byzantine underground cistern, with seemingly endless rows of columns, was built to supply water to Emperor Justinian's Great Palace and the gardens in the 6C.

The Bosphorus★★
Take a boat trip along this most beautiful of waterways, which separates both the city and two continents, and joins the Black Sea to the Sea of Marmara. Its shores are lined with summer palaces and grand embassies, including the splendour of the Dolmabahçe Palace, home to the last Sultans.

City Walls★
Running from the Golden Horn to the Sea of Marmara, and described as the 'most effective fortification ever', Theodosius' 5C walls bear the battle scars of endless waves of attackers.

TOPKAPI PALACE★★★

This walk explores the gardens and pavilions of the Topkapı Palace, and provides plenty to occupy even the most ardent of sightseers for a full day. It was Sultan Mehmet the Conqueror who established the **Topkapı Sarayı** (Topkapı Palace) on Saray Burnu (Palace Point) shortly after the Conquest of the city in the 15C. Over the centuries, successive sultans altered and added to the palace, but it remained the residence of the greatest sultans and centre of the Ottoman Empire for nearly 400 years, until Abdül Mecit moved to the Dolmabahçe Palace on the shores of the Bosphorus in the 1850s.

It may appear a veritable hotchpotch of buildings linked by a maze of courtyards and passageways, but in reality the palace complex is laid out in a meticulously logical manner. There are four **courtyards**,

The twin towers of the Gate of Salutations lead to the second courtyard of Topkapı Palace.

progressing from more public ones through to the most private areas. The first (outer) courtyard was open to all, and contained many of the palace's most basic services. The second courtyard was devoted to the **Divan**, the Council of State, where decisions affecting the whole empire were debated. The third courtyard was largely taken up by the palace school. The fourth was the private domain of the sultan and his retinue, where the serious business of state gave way to more enjoyable aspects of life.

Today's visitors enter the complex through the **Bab-ı Hümayün** (the Imperial Gate). Before entering, take time to admire the **Ahmet III Çeşmesi** (fountain of Sultan Ahmet III), built in 1728 in handsome Ottoman rococo style.

Crossing the first courtyard, the **Bab-üs Selam** (Gate of Salutations), better known as the Orta Kapı or Middle Gate, leads through to the second courtyard. Here, the gardens are planted with ancient cypress and plane trees, underplanted with beds of roses, once irrigated with water from the great Byzantine cistern of Yerebatan Sarayı (Basilica Cistern). Along the right hand side of the courtyard are the ten **palace kitchens**, partly reconstructed by Sinan, and once served by a staff of 1 500. Today, most of the kitchens house a stunning **collection of porcelain**, much of Chinese origin, dating from the 10C-

The lavishly decorated entrance to the 16C Imperial Chamber.

19C. Two rooms remain much as they did in Ottoman times, with a remarkable array of kitchen utensils, most of a monumental size.

Along the left hand side of the courtyard lie the Divan, with its distinctive tower (not open to the public), the **Treasury** (displaying fine, yet barbaric weapons of war), and the **Harem★★**. The harem can only be visited on a whistlestop, guided tour, which runs every hour. This is heavily booked, so it is well worth getting a ticket on arrival, before looking round the rest of the palace. The harem comprises a vast complex maze of passages, chambers (over 300 in all), courtyards and gardens, all on a surprisingly small and intimate scale. The word *harem* means 'forbidden': here the sultan kept his wives, female servants (*odalisques*), and children, together with the Black Eunuchs, who were in charge of the harem's day-to-day running. At its most crowded, the harem employed over 400 *odalisques*, under the charge of several hundred eunuchs. However, the most influential individual in the harem was the Valide Sultan, the mother of the reigning sultan, most of whom were experts in political intrigue. Here, too, was the infamous **Kafes** ('Cage'), where the younger brothers of a reigning sultan were incarcerated to avoid the possibility of a war of succession. The years spent in the Cage were blamed for the insanity of many of the sultans.

Only a few rooms of the harem are currently open to the public, but these include some of the most beautiful, such as the 16C apartments of the **Hünkar Odası** (Hall of the Emperor or Imperial Chamber), the **Salon of Murat III** (1578)

The Imperial Chamber of the harem is beautifully decorated with tiles. It was probably designed by the great Ottoman architect, Sinan.

and the **Dining Room of Ahmet III** (1706).

The **Bab-üs Saadet** (Gate of Felicity) leads into the third courtyard. Immediately in front stands the **Arz Odası** (Throne Room), where the sultan awaited the outcome of the Divan session in order to give his assent to their proposals.

To the right of the courtyard lies the **Pavilion of the Conqueror**, which houses the **Topkapı Treasury★★★**, an incomparable collection of treasures, from the exquisitely beautiful to the grotesque. Among jewel-encrusted thrones and jewel-studded pendants, are the **Topkapı Dagger**, studded with three giant emeralds, and star of the Peter Ustinov classic *Topkapı*; the **Spoonmaker's Diamond**, an 86-carat giant (the fifth largest in the world), that adorned the turban of Mehmet IV; and golden reliquaries, supposedly containing fragments of the **skull and hand of St John the Baptist**.

Across the courtyard from the Conqueror's Pavilion stands the **Pavilion of the Holy Mantle**, containing venerated relics from the Prophet Mohammed himself. These include a footprint, hair and tooth of the Prophet, as well as his mantle, brought home by Sultan Selim the Grim after his conquest of Egypt in 1517.

Lying between the two pavilions, on the north-east side of the courtyard, are the former **Treasurer's Quarters**, which today display part of the vast **Collection of Paintings and Miniatures** dating from the reign of Sultan Süleyman the Magnificent to that of Ahmet III.

A small passageway to the left of the miniatures collection leads into the fourth courtyard, with its fine pavilions and pools set in beautiful gardens. Here the sultans revelled. Most notorious of all was Sultan İbrahim I (İbrahim the Mad), who at the culmination of his reign ordered the drowning of all 280 concubines from his harem, following a fit of sexual jealousy. Take time to visit the small yet delightful **Bağdad Köşkü**, **İftariye Köşkü** and **Sünnet Odası** (Circumcision Room), before passing to the **Mecidiye Köşkü** for a drink and to admire the fine panorama of the city.

Around the Topkapı Palace

Returning to the outer courtyard, a few other attractions are well worth a visit, but if the palace has overwhelmed you, visit them on another day. To the right of the Imperial Gate of the outer walls stands the church of **Aya İrini★** (Church of Divine Peace), the

second largest Byzantine church surviving in the city today, and the second of three to be built by the prolific Emperor Justinian in AD 537, on the site of earlier sanctuaries. The building takes the form of a basilica with dome, but unfortunately is generally closed to the public, except when it forms the venue for performances during the mid-summer International Music Festival. Immediately beyond the church is the **Darphane-ı Amire** (Imperial Mint).

A small roadway to the right of the Imperial Mint leads down to the **Archaeological Museum complex★★★**, and ultimately the Gülhane Park. On passing through the main gateway into the museums' central courtyard, the **Eski Şark Eserleri Müzesi** (Museum of the Ancient Orient) stands immediately on the left. This contains a remarkable collection of artifacts from pre-Islamic Egypt, Mesopotamia and Asia Minor, many of quite exceptional historic importance. Amongst the most treasured accessions are: **tile panels** from the time of Babylonian King Nebuchadnezzar (604-562 BC), with blue and yellow animal

One of the renowned tile panels of a lion, dating from around the 6C BC, in the Museum of the Ancient Orient.

reliefs; the famous **Code of Hammurabi**, Babylonian laws from around 1750 BC; and a clay tablet recording the **Treaty of Kadesh** (1269 BC) between Pharaoh Rameses II and the Hittite King Hattusilas, the oldest peace treaty known to mankind (a copy now decorates the entrance to the United Nations building in New York).

The main building of the complex is the **Arkeoloji Müzesi** (Archaeological Museum), which was given the European Council of Museums Award in 1993. The right wing contains the museum's superb collection of **Greco-Roman antiquities**, principally from classical sites in Turkey. Amongst the most notable exhibits are the **statue of Ephebos of Tralles** (3C BC), the **head of Alexander the Great** (3C BC copy of Lysippus original), and the **head of Emperor Arcadius**, found in Beyazit Square. The left wing contains the museum's most celebrated items, the incomparably beautiful **sarcophagi** excavated in 1887 from the royal burial ground at Sidon by Osman Hamdi Bey, Turkey's leading archaeologist, and

A detail of a Greek relief illustrating the struggle of Athena and Gigantes (AD 2C), from the Archaeological Museum.

including the so-called **Alexander Sarcophagus** (4C BC) and the **Sarcophagus of the Mourning Widows** (around 350 BC). The first floor of the museum houses a display depicting **İstanbul Through the Ages**, which concentrates on the pre-Ottoman city. Among its exhibits, many from Byzantine structures now destroyed, are **one of the heads of the Serpent Column** and a few links of the **chain** with which the Byzantines closed the Bosphorus to enemies.

The third building in the complex is the **Çinili Köşk** (the Tiled Pavilion) which houses a fine collection of **Turkish ceramics**, including examples from the celebrated kilns at İznik. The building itself is of considerable interest, for it is one of the oldest (1472) secular buildings in the city, built by Sultan Mehmet the Conqueror as a peaceful retreat.

An imperial Byzantine sarcophagus outside the Archaeological Museum.

AROUND THE HIPPODROME

This second walk concentrates on the area immediately around the Hippodrome, and visits many of the city's principal monuments, as well as many lesser sights.

Ayasofya★★★ (Haghia Sophia, The Church of the Divine Wisdom)

Few buildings have played such a pivotal role as Ayasofya, or Haghia Sophia, which crowns the First Hill and has inspired wonderment among past and present travellers alike. In fact, the structure standing today was the third to be built on the site. Both the first and second – built by Emperor Constantius II at the behest of his father Constantine the Great, and by Emperor Theodosius II – were burnt to the ground during periods of rioting. Theodosius' church was razed during the **Nika Riots** of AD 532 in the reign of **Justinian**. The rioters were shown no mercy by the emperor – 30 000 were trapped in the Hippodrome and slaughtered under Justinian's orders – and Justinian lost no time in rebuilding the church (and much of the city) on a scale altogether grander than before. On 23 February 532 (just 39 days after the destruction of its predecessor) the first stone of the new church was laid.

Justinian chose **Anthemius of Tralles** and **Isidore of Miletus** (both from Aegean Turkey) as architects for his new church. The choice was inspired. The design was revolutionary and the resulting church was the largest religious building in the Christian world at the time, and so it remained until the 15C. The interior was decorated with the most valuable materials and housed a formidable array of venerated

Ayasofya is one of the great landmarks of İstanbul.

relics, including the True Cross, Jesus' swaddling clothes, and the table upon which Jesus and disciples reputedly ate their last supper together (all sent back from Jerusalem by the ever-industrious Empress Helena, mother of Constantine the Great). Little wonder that Justinian was awed by its magnificence on completion: 'Glory to God who has deemed me worthy of accomplishing such a work! Solomon, I have surpassed thee.' The church had taken just five years, ten months and four days to complete.

Today's visitors enter the church through the same doorway used by Justinian over 1 400 years ago. The **exonarthex** and **narthex** (outer and inner hallways) lead through the **Imperial Gate** into the main body of the building. The domed structure has a square ground plan. To the left and right are two side aisles, above which lie the **galleries**. It is the sheer scale of the church which impresses. The **dome** is 32m (105ft) in diameter, and soars 55m (180ft) above the floor. The supporting drum on which the dome sits is pierced by 40 windows, admitting light to the building and making the dome itself appear as if 'suspended from heaven by a gold chain'. Many of the walls are still clad with **marble panels** of the finest quality and variety, while a number of the church's columns were raided from classical sites across the Byzantine empire. These are topped with exquisitely carved marble capitals.

The **mosaics** are the most impressive feature of the interior decoration. On completion, it seems that all surfaces not faced with marble were covered with gold mosaics, or rich red, green and blue mosaics in simple geometric designs. They once covered an area of 20 000m^2 (215 282ft^2) and much still survives today. 'The golden stream of glittering rays pour down and strike the eyes of men, so that they can scarcely bear to look,' eulogised one contemporary chronicler. The figurative mosaics were added at a later date. Among the most beautiful are: the **mosaic of Leo VI** (about AD 900, lunette above Imperial Gate in narthex); the **mosaic of the Virgin Mary with infant Christ** (*c.*867, conch of apse); **the Deisis**, depicting Christ flanked by the Blessed Virgin and St John the Baptist (second half of the 13C, far end of south gallery); the **mosaic of the Emperor John II Comnenus and the Empress Eirene** offering

The Deisis from the 13C, although partly damaged, is still a magnificent sight.

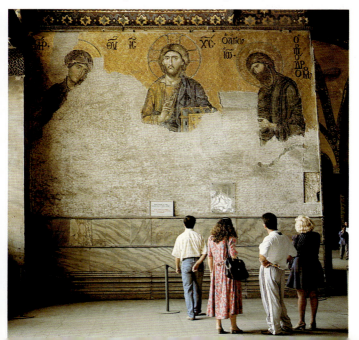

A mosaic showing Christ flanked by Constantine IX and the Empress Zoe.

a bag of money and a scroll to the infant Christ in the arms of the Virgin Mary (1118, far end of south gallery); and a dedicatory **mosaic of Constantine the Great and Justinian** offering models of the city and the great church respectively to the infant Jesus (around 1000, lunette above door leading from Vestibule of Warriors into the narthex).

Of the Byzantine furnishings little remains. Much was destroyed or carted away during the orgy of destruction by the Christians during the Fourth Crusade, in June 1204. History repeated itself on 29 May 1453, when the victorious Ottomans ransacked the church. However, when Mehmet the Conqueror himself later arrived, he ordered that the church be converted into a mosque. The first Muslim service was held three days later. Accordingly, a number of notable Ottoman decorative elements still survive, including two 2m (7ft) high **alabaster urns** (either side of the Imperial Gate); the **four medallions**

The pillars in the vast interior of Ayasofya are decorated with plaques bearing gilded sacred inscriptions in Arabic.

with gold inscriptions bearing sacred Islamic names (believed to be the largest examples of Arabic calligraphy), situated in the four corners of the nave; the free-standing **muezzin's tribune**; the **Sultan's loge** and **minber** (left and right of the apse); and the **mihrab** niche indicating the direction of Mecca. Ayasofya was last used as a mosque in the 1930s. It is currently undergoing extensive restoration.

Ayasofya is surrounded by other buildings and structures of interest, most notably a few **foundations of the Theodosian church**, and a series of **imperial Ottoman tombs**, including one of Sinan's most beautiful works, the Tomb of Selim II.

Leaving the precinct of Ayasofya, the multi-domed building to the left is the **Haseki Hürrem Hamamı** (the baths of Roxelana), commissioned by Sultan Süleyman the Magnificent for his wife. Beautifully restored, the fine double baths now serve as a carpet museum and showroom.

The Blue Mosque with its six graceful minarets.

Sultan Ahmet Camii★★★ (Blue Mosque)

The other building dominating the skyline here is the Blue Mosque, the most renowned mosque in the city. Sultan Ahmet I commissioned the architect Mehmet Ağa, a student of the great Sinan, to build the mosque, which was completed in 1616. From the outside it is a most pleasingly proportioned building, with a series of fine domes and semi-domes, and a handsome courtyard, the whole accentuated by the six graceful minarets. One writer records how the six minarets were adorned by 12 000 lamps 'so that they resembled as many fiery cypresses'. The more pious were less admiring, considering the minarets to be sacrilegious, for until this date only the Great Mosque at Mecca had six.

The mosque's interior is light and airy: 260 windows, formerly filled with stained glass from Venice, let in copious light which falls on predominately blue paintwork and İznik tiles, giving rise to the popular name, Blue Mosque. The tiles – all 20 000 of them – are particularly splendid, being fired in İznik towards the end of its heyday as a tile-producing town. Ahmet banned others from ordering tiles from the kilns while his mosque was under construction. His mania for tilework put heavy demands on the kilns and, it is said, was responsible for the industry's subsequent decline. Other features in the mosque are the fine inlay woodwork of the doors and window shutters, and the metalwork. If anything detracts from the grace of the interior, it is the four colossal columns supporting the dome and semi-domes: each is 5m (16ft) in diameter.

Two small museums are worth a visit at this stage in the walk. The **Hünkâr Kasrı**

The sumptuous tiled interior of the Blue Mosque.

(Royal Pavilion) of the mosque (situated at its south-east corner) houses a **Carpet Museum**, with priceless examples from across Anatolia, some dating back to the 13C. Many have been retrieved from the floors of the country's older mosques and associated warehouses.

On the slopes below the mosque lies the restored **Arasta Çarşısı,** a bazaar built to provide revenue for the mosque's upkeep. Today, this row of shops mainly deals in carpets and kilims. Halfway along this street, a small entrance leads down into the **Mosaic Museum**, one of the few remains of the Great Palace, home to so many of the Byzantine emperors. Thought to date from around AD 500, these vividly coloured mosaics depict animals, hunting scenes, chariot races and mythological figures.

At Meydanı (Hippodrome)

Adjacent to the inner courtyard of the Blue Mosque is the site of the Hippodrome, the focal point of civil activities in Byzantine times. The Hippodrome was laid out by **Emperor Septimius Severus** in AD 203, and was later enlarged by **Constantine the Great**. Measuring 480m (1 575ft) long, 120m (394ft) wide, and with seating 30 to 40 rows in depth, it is estimated that the Hippodrome could seat 100 000 spectators.

Today, the floor of the Hippodrome lies buried under nearly 5m (16ft) of soil and a road runs round the track once used by chariots, but the visitor can still view three of the numerous columns and obelisks that formerly adorned the central spine of the racetrack. The others, including four magnificent bronze gilt horses by Lysippus, were carried off to Venice and elsewhere by the Crusaders.

The **Egyptian Obelisk**, rising to about 30m (98ft) and covered with hieroglyphic pictograms, was originally commissioned by Pharaoh Thutmose III in the mid 15C BC. During shipment to Constantinople in the 4C AD, it broke into pieces, and the section standing today represents only the top third. The granite ornamentation is as clear as the

Detail of the hieroglyphics on the Egyptian Obelisk in the Hippodrome.

day it was carved, in stark contrast to the images of Emperor Theodosius I that adorn the limestone plinth on which the obelisk stands.

The **Serpent Column** was originally commissioned by 31 Greek city-states as an offering of thanks to Apollo, following their victory over Persians in battle. Constantine brought it from Delphi to Constantinople in AD 326, at which time it comprised the bodies of three intertwined snakes, supporting a golden cauldron. Today, the heads and cauldron have gone, although one of the heads was later recovered and is on display in the Archaeological Museum.

The **Column of Constantine Porphyrogenitus**, the unadorned column standing 32m (105ft) high, was probably erected by Theodosius I or Constantine the Great. Emperor Constantine VII Porphyrogenitus was responsible for cladding the pillar in bronze, but this fell prey to the light-fingered Crusaders, who smelted it down to make coins.

Dominating the north-western side of the Hippodrome is the **Palace of İbrahim Paşa**, today home to the **Türk ve İslam Eserleri Müzesi** (Museum of Turkish and Islamic Art). The palace was built for İbrahim Paşa in 1524 and represents the largest and one of the finest private residences to be constructed in Ottoman İstanbul. The Paşa himself was Grand Vezir to Sultan Süleyman the Magnificent for 13 years, before he fell out of favour and was duly strangled while sleeping, by order of his master. The museum houses a fine and extensive collection of carpets, manuscripts, calligraphy, ceramics, metalwork and an ethnographical collection (notably

The Serpent Column and the Egyptian Obelisk in the Hippodrome.

The Basilica Cistern at one time irrigated the gardens of the Topkapı Palace. The roof is supported by 336 columns.

displaying black goat-hair tents and other artifacts of the Anatolian nomads, who even today wander across Turkey's high plateaux). The museum was awarded a European Council-UNESCO award in 1985.

Finally, returning towards Ayasofya, save some energy to visit the **Yerebatan Sarayı**★★ (Basilica Cistern or Underground Palace), undoubtedly the city's finest surviving underground water cistern, and certainly one of its oddest monuments. Built by Emperor Justinian in 532 to counter increasing water shortages at the nearby Great Palace, its waters were later diverted to irrigate the gardens of the Topkapı Palace, before falling into disuse. Rediscovered by French traveller Petrus Gyllius in the 16C, today's visitors can share some his wonderment on descending into its cavernous void. Magnificently restored, the vaulted brick roof is supported by 336 columns, each 12m (40ft) tall, and topped by a variety of capitals, raided from earlier buildings around the First Hill. Particularly fine is a column with the distinctive 'peacock eye' design (similar to ones to be seen in the Forum of Theodosius, and called the 'Tear Column'), and two huge carved heads of Medusa, today relegated to supporting columns at the far left corner of the cistern.

A Medusa head supporting one of the Cistern's pillars was probably brought by Justinian from the ancient city of Chalcedon.

THE MARKET QUARTER

The third walk explores the area which has been the principal market quarter since Byzantine times, hugging the slopes below the Second Hill down to the shores of the Golden Horn. The walk starts in Beyazit Square.

Beyazit Meydanı★ (Beyazit Square) bustles with students and street vendors, the latter selling everything from sherbet drinks and pigeon grain, to designer jeans and Byzantine relics, though perhaps some of dubious origin. Small cafés offer snacks and soft drinks in the shade of towering plane trees.

Dominating the square is **Beyazit Camii** (Mosque of Beyazit II), completed in 1506. It is the oldest surviving great imperial mosque in the city, following the destruction by earthquake of the original Fatih Mehmet Camii (Mosque of Mehmet the Conqueror). It is a handsome mosque, with a particularly fine inner courtyard, a ground plan similar to that of Ayasofya (with a large central dome, and semi-domes at its north and south ends), and lovely interior furnishings, including the marble minber, royal loge, muezzin's tribune, and carved wooden doors. Also notable are the mosque's two minarets, positioned at the end of projecting wings and purportedly the most widely spaced in Islam. To the east of the mosque, a small passageway leads into the **Sahaflar Çarşısı** (the Market of Secondhand

The lively Beyazit Square is overlooked by the Mosque of Beyazıt II.

The famous Grand Bazaar houses a colourful maze of around 4 000 shops in its narrow passageways.

Booksellers), set in a charming shaded courtyard and surrounded by over 40 stalls selling books, old and new, as well as modern-day facsimiles of historic Ottoman miniature paintings, which fool many a treasure hunter.

On leaving the book bazaar at its far end, the **Kapalı Çarşı★★★** (Grand Bazaar) looms in front of the visitor. This is the most famous of the oriental covered bazaars, and it is easy to get disorientated among its 4 000 shops and its maze of 60 streets, not to mention teahouses, banks, mosques and baths. Quite the best option is just to let the bazaar engulf you and your senses, and enjoy its unforgettable sights and sounds.

As with most market areas in the city, different types of trade are concentrated in different parts of the market: you will find streets and markets of goldsmiths and pearl-merchants, carpets, souvenirs and antiques, as well as the rather more extraordinary fez-makers and curers of beef (*pastırmacı*). Be sure to search out the **Cevahir** or **İç Bedesten** (Old Bedesten) in the centre of the bazaar, and the **Sandal Bedesteni** to its east. These represent the oldest sections of the bazaar, dating back to the times of Sultan Mehmet the Conqueror and Sultan Beyazit II respectively, and are particularly fine, with their multi-domed roofs.

To the east of the Grand Bazaar lies the idiosyncratic **Nuruosmaniye Camii** (Mosque of the Sacred Light of Osman), lying within a picturesque outer courtyard shaded by plane and lime trees. The mosque was the first to be built in the new Ottoman baroque style, and was completed in 1755 by a little-known Greek architect called Simeon. If you get the opportunity, look round the outside of its unique horseshoe-shaped inner courtyard, for you will be rewarded with a splendid view over the roof-tops of the bazaar.

Around the bazaar lies a constellation of small **hans** (workshops), each alive from dawn to dusk with the sounds of looms, presses and blacksmiths' hammers. If the Grand Bazaar is where the merchants sell their wares, this is where they are made. If you have an old but worn carpet that needs repairing, or a suit that needs re-tailoring, or perhaps a brochure to be printed, this is where you come.

Some of the oldest and finest of the hans lie immediately to the east of Uzun Çarşı

Caddesi, and are well worth searching out, both for their atmosphere and architecture. Each bears its name above the main entrance, so look out for **Büyük Yeni Han** (the Big New Market, 1764) and **Büyük Valide Hanı★** (the market of Sultan Valide Kösem, 1651). In both, unassailable studded iron-clad doors lead into courtyards bounded by handsome tiered arcades.

Returning to Uzun Çarşı Caddesi, the road drops rapidly to the Golden Horn, becoming increasingly narrow and gridlocked as cars, vans, vendors and porters all try to force themselves past one another in impossibly crowded streets. Here, too, the trades are segregated: traders in leatherware and briefcases at the top give way to dealers

A tailor working in one of the hans around the Grand Bazaar.

The sights and smells of the street market below the royal pavilion of Yeni Cami, with its cosmopolitan range of spices and foods, make it well worth a visit.

in shotguns and brassware, before passing into makers of coathangers, broom handles and hammocks.

At the end of the street, the small, yet beautiful, **Rüstem Paşa Camii**★★ (Mosque of Rüstem Paşa) sits proud on its own raised terrace above the shops. Rüstem Paşa himself was a little-loved Grand Vezir of Sultan Süleyman, whose only saving grace was his love of fine buildings. This mosque was built for the vezir in 1561, yet another of the masterful works of architect Sinan. It is accessed by enclosed stairways that lead up to its distinctive double porchway. The walls below the porch bear panels of exquisite **İznik tiles**, yet these are but a foretaste of the rich decoration to be found inside the mosque. Clearly, Rüstem Paşa's motto in life was that it was impossible to have too much of a good thing, for virtually every interior surface is covered with tiles of the very best quality.

Returning to the end of Uzun Çarşı Caddesi, a right turn brings you into a road that ultimately ends at the **Mısır Çarşısı**★ (Egyptian or Spice Bazaar). Inside, the sights, sounds and smells almost overwhelm the senses. In shop after shop, sacks of spices, nuts, dried fruit and potions jostle with one another for your attention: this is a good place to buy saffron from Spain or India, caviar from Iran, herbal teas collected from the steppes of Anatolia, and perhaps even a jar of aphrodisiac of the sultan, doubtless concocted behind the scenes in the bazaar. The building itself is of historic importance, constructed for **Hatice Turhan Sultan** (mother of Mehmet IV) in 1660 to provide revenue for the upkeep of the nearby Yeni Cami.

The İstanbul Tulip

According to the oral traditions of the Prophet Mohammed, people will do in their afterlife what they most enjoyed during their time on earth. As flowers belong in heaven, so gardeners can be assured of going to heaven to continue their work.

The Ottomans were exceptionally fond of flowers and gardening. The 1550s not only saw the development of an all-powerful empire, but also saw a renaissance in all forms of arts and architecture. Nowhere was this more evident than in İstanbul. Favourite flowers among Ottoman gardeners were roses, narcissi, hyacinths and carnations, but most cherished of all was the tulip, believed to be a symbol of God (for its name – *lale* – is written using the same Arabic letters as 'Allah') and of modesty (for when in full bloom, the tulip bows its head).

We can get an idea of what the İstanbul Tulip looked like, for their image appears on a multitude of objects during the 16C-18C, including textiles and clothing, embroidered prayer rugs, painted wall decorations, miniature illustrations, carved marble fountain façades and ceramics. During the 16C, the İstanbul Tulip looked rather similar to the modern-day varieties from Holland, but over the next two centuries the Ottomans selected and bred their prized blooms with undisguised zeal. This humble flower reached its peak in popularity during the 'Lale Devri' – the Tulip Period of Sultan Ahmet III, in the early decades of the 18C. By this time, over 1 500 varieties had been named, selected for blooms with almond-shaped petals, their tips narrowed into long, fine dagger-like points. Names such as Flirtatious, Light of Happiness, Slim one of the Rose Garden and Glitter of Prosperity all hint at the high esteem in which the tulip was held. During this period, councils of learned florists judged new varieties: only the most perfect were deemed worthy to bear a name. In an attempt to curb rocketing prices, the State even published annual lists of fixed prices.

Yet fashions change, and the tulip declined into obscurity in the second half of the 18C. Of the 1 500 varieties so lovingly grown and named, not a single one survives today. But for today's visitor, images of this flower once so special to İstanbul can still be seen, a reminder of an extraordinary episode in the city's long history.

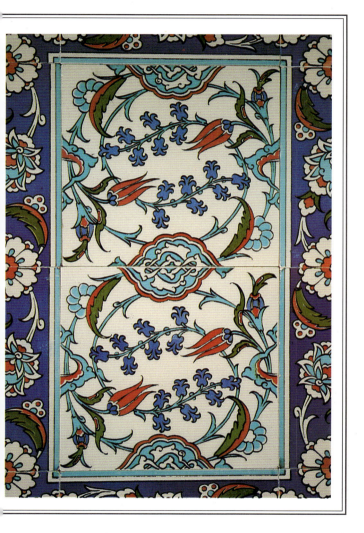

OTHER ATTRACTIONS

Askeri Müze★
(Military Museum) [Map: CX]
Founded in 1959 and housed in the former Military Academy gymnasium, the Military Museum houses a fine collection of weapons, uniforms and other equipment, largely from the Ottoman period. Notable exhibits include uniforms of the Janissaries (elite fighting corp), luxurious imperial campaign tents, and some of the links of chain with which the Byzantines closed the mouth of the Golden Horn. The museum is worth visiting just to experience the Janissary marching band, which plays between 3-4pm on days when the museum is open.

Beyoğlu (Pera) [Map: BY & CY]
Attracted by its exotic culture, westerners have settled the Pera district of İstanbul for centuries, giving this district a European flavour all of its own. From the middle of the 19C, the district became the real social, political and economic centre of the city. With boulevards bearing names such as the **Grande Rue de Pera★** (today's **İstiklal Caddesi**), and lined with fine mansions and embassies, the area took on a graceful air quite unique in the oriental city. A walk from **Taksim Square** along İstiklal Caddesi is well worth the time spent. Embassies hide behind fine iron gateways, and privately-owned shopping arcades have been converted into nightclubs and alleys full of shops, market stalls and taverns, whilst still retaining much of their architectural grace. Perhaps the most famous and attractive of these is **Çiçek Pasajı,** once a flower market

Boarding one of the refurbished trams in Beyoğlu.

but now a lively glass-roofed arcade of restaurants and beer parlours, throbbing with music and local colour.

Gone are the smoke-belching cars, replaced by the historic trams that have been brought out of storage to serve this area once more. Do not miss the vibrant **Balık Pazarı** (fish market), nor the elegant grace of the **Pera Palas Hotel** (in the parallel Meşrutiyet Caddesi). The hotel was built in the late 19C to accommodate increasing numbers of European tourists, many of whom would arrive here after a trip on the *Orient Express* (*see* p.98). At the southern end is **Tünel**, one of the shortest and oldest underground railways in the world, built by French engineers in 1875, and which carries passengers from İstiklal Caddesi to sea level.

The elegant interior of the Pera Palas Hotel.

Outside the tomb of Eyüp el-Ensari. The walls are covered in a bewildering array of tiles.

Bozdoğan Kemeri★
(Valens Aqueduct) [Map: AZ]
Bestriding the valley between İstanbul's Third and Fourth Hills, Emperor Valens' double-arched aqueduct remains one of the most distinctive landmarks in the city, built around AD 370. It formed part of the longest 'Roman' water-supply network in existence, which carried water from Turkish Thrace, a distance of 242km (150 miles). Originally over 1000m (3 280ft) long, only 625m (2 050ft) remains intact.

Column of Constantine [Map: BX]
Built by Constantine the Great to commemorate the founding of the new capital of the Roman Empire in AD 330, the column was originally crowned by a statue of Constantine and stood in the oval Forum of Constantine. The statue was toppled in a hurricane in 1106, and only 35m (115ft) of the column remains, supported with iron bands, yet it still has the power to impress.

Eyüp [Map:AX]

Eyüp contains the holiest Islamic shrine in İstanbul, for it is here that Eyüp el-Ensari – close friend and standard-bearer of the Prophet Mohammad – is supposedly buried, following his death during the first Arab siege of İstanbul in AD 668-669. His imposing **tomb** lies within the courtyard of the **Eyüp Sultan Külliyesi**★ (the mosque complex of Eyüp Sultan), which was one of the first Ottoman mosque complexes to be built in İstanbul after the 1453 siege, though later rebuilt in 1800 by Sultan Selim III, following earthquake damage. The mosque is a beautiful example of the Ottoman baroque style.

Other splendid mosques occur around the village (including Sinan's innovative **Zal Mahmut Paşa Camii**) and are worth a visit, as are the shady graveyards and the **café of Pierre Loti**, favoured by the famous French writer for its incomparable **views**★★ of the city.

There are excellent views of the Golden Horn from the café of Pierre Loti.

A detail from the interior of the Mosque of Mehemet the Conqueror.

Fatih Mehmet Camii
(Mosque of Mehmet the Conqueror) [Map:AY]

'The Sultan himself selected the best site...and commanded them to erect there a mosque which...should vie with the largest and finest of the temples already existing there [i.e. Ayasofya].' For Mehmet the Conqueror, the architect Atık Sinan created a complex (*külliye*) of buildings without parallel in the Ottoman world at that time. The mosque itself incorporated a dome 26m (85ft) in width, but this was narrower than that of Ayasofya, so the displeased Sultan ordered the execution of his luckless architect. An earthquake in 1766 destroyed the mosque (replaced in 1771), but other original buildings of the *külliye* survive.

Fethiye Camii★ (Church of the Theotokos Pammakaristos) [Map:AY]
This lovely 12C Byzantine church is in three sections, much altered over time, and stands on a terrace overlooking the Golden Horn. It is most noted for its mosaics in the funerary chapel; these are contemporary to those in the better-known Kariye Camii, and while not so numerous, are nevertheless of exceptional beauty in their own right (mainly depicting Christ, together with saints and patriarchs). Check with a tourist information office about opening hours.

İmrahor Camii (Church of St John of Studius) [Map: not shown, about 500m/1 640ft inside Land Walls. Building not open, but the local

keeper will usually open the gate to visitors.]
Founded in 463, this is the oldest Byzantine
church in İstanbul, built by the Eastern
Consul Studius on the simple basilica plan.
The most venerated relic in the church was
the severed head of St John the Baptist, and
each year on the anniversary of his
beheading, the Byzantine Emperors would
visit the church on pilgrimage. The church
was originally attached to a monastery,
whose monks were known as *Akoimetai* – the
insomniacs – for they prayed in shifts
around the clock. By the 9C, the monastery
had become the most powerful in the
Empire, and a centre of scholarship and
artistic excellence. Today the monastery no
longer stands, and the church is merely a
shell, victim to fire, earthquake and raiding
by Crusaders in the 13C (who stole, amongst
other things, the Baptist's head). Yet even in
this state, it remains an impressive structure.

A ruined shell is all that remains of the Byzantine Church of St John of Studius, part of the most powerful monastery in the empire.

Kariye Camii*** (St Saviour in Chora)
[Map:AY]

The modest exterior of this small, yet handsome, Byzantine church gives no clue to the wealth of exquisite mosaics and frescoes to be found inside, dating from the last (Palaeologian) renaissance in Byzantine art. The current church dates from the late 11C, and was greatly altered over the following two centuries. The last major reconstruction was undertaken by **Theodore Metochites**, First Lord of the Treasury, who completely redecorated the interior as we see it today, during the period 1315-1321. Following the Conquest, the church was

St Saviour in Chora houses some of the finest Byzantine mosaics and frescoes, such as this one of the Blessed Virgin and Christ Child.

converted to a mosque during the reign of Sultan Beyazit II, and the interior decorations plastered over. The mosaics and frescoes, depicting nearly 300 scenes from Jesus' life, were uncovered by the Byzantine Institute of America from 1948 to 1958, and the church is now a museum displaying some of the world's finest Byzantine mosaics and frescoes.

The Maiden's Tower is built on the site of an earlier fortification which may have held one end of a chain which protected the Bosphorus.

Kız Kulesi (Maiden's Tower or Leander's Tower) [Map: DY]

Situated on a rocky outcrop at the mouth of the Bosphorus, this 30m (98ft) tower is a prominent landmark in the city, built in 1763 to replace earlier structures dating back to Byzantine times. Its name 'Maiden's Tower' comes from the legend of a sultan's

daughter who lived here in isolation, fearing that she would die of snakebite on the mainland. Even here, she was not safe from the jaws of death, for a snake reached the island in a basket of fruit and promptly bit her. The tower is not open to the public.

Küçük Ayasofya★ (Church of SS Sergius and Bacchus) [Map: BZ]

This delightful small church was built by the ever-prolific Emperor Justinian in 530, in honour of the two patron saints of the army, Sergius and Bacchus. Whilst formerly adorned with an abundance of gold mosaic and marble revetments which 'outshone the sun', the church's interior still charms, with its beautiful columns of green verd-antique and red Synnada marbles, topped with finely carved marble capitals.

Lâleli Camii (Tulip Mosque)
[Map: AZ, off Ordu Caddesi]

The last great mosque complex to be built in the city by the sultans (completed in 1763 by Sultan Mustafa III), the Tulip Mosque is widely regarded as a fine example of the baroque style.

City Walls★ [Map: partly shown in AX & AY]

Theodosius II constructed the mighty land walls in the first half of the 5C to resist attack from the city's landward boundary. They originally ran for 6.6km (4 miles) in a great arc, linking the Sea of Marmara to the Golden Horn. The walls were a formidable fortification, made up of a moat and immense outer and inner walls, each with 96 towers from which the terrible 'Greek Fire' (burning oil) was hurled.

Visitors to the walls should not miss the

The mighty 5C City Walls are still an impressive sight today.

One of the towers of the fortress of Yedikule.

fortress of **Yedikule** (Castle of Seven Towers), near the shores of the Sea of Marmara. Here, by the addition of three extra towers, Sultan Mehmet the Conqueror created a fine fortress shortly after the Conquest. At first used as an arsenal and treasury, its huge towers were later used as a prison for unwanted sultans and grand vezirs.

The castle walls also incorporated the monumental **Golden Gate**, the triumphal arch through which so many victorious emperors paraded after success in battle. Towards the northern end of the land walls, the remains of late Byzantine palaces (11C-14C) can be seen at **Tekfur Sarayı** and the **Palace of Blachernae**.

Şehzade Camii (Prince's Mosque)
[Map: AZ, off Şehzade Başı Caddesi]
Sultan Süleyman the Magnificent commissioned this mosque in memory of his beloved son Mehmet, who succumbed to smallpox in his early twenties. It is an enigmatic mosque, built by the empire's most celebrated architect, Sinan, in his apprentice days, and completed in 1548. Perhaps the most beautiful features of the complex are the tombs in the mosque garden, decorated in beautiful tilework, where Rüstem Paşa, İbrahim Paşa and, of course, the prince himself are buried.

Sokollu Mehmet Paşa Camii★
(Mosque of Sokollu Mehmet Paşa) [Map: ZB]
Small, yet beautifully proportioned, this mosque is a minor masterpiece by architect Sinan. Amongst its great attractions are its interior decorations, which include fragments of black stone from the venerated Kaaba, in Mecca, and a stunning panel of İznik tiles down the mihrab wall.

Süleymaniye Camii★★★
(Mosque of Sultan Süleyman the Magnificent)
[Map: BZ]
The mosque complex is the finest in İstanbul, constructed for the most powerful sultan by architect Sinan, and completed in

1557. Situated on the slopes above the Golden Horn, the mosque stands proud above a vast complex of other pious foundations and institutions. What impresses the visitor most is the sheer size of the mosque itself, modelled on the church of Ayasofya. The magnificent dome is 26m (85ft) in diameter, and soars 52m (171ft) above the floor of the building. The interior decoration is used with restraint, and greatly enhances the beauty of this lovely mosque: tilework on the mihrab wall, original paintwork, and stained-glass windows are all of the finest craftsmanship.

Sultan Süleyman and his wife, Roxelana,

The octagonal mausoleum housing the tomb of Süleyman was designed by Sinan. The walls are covered with exquisite Iznik tiles. A great turban, appropriate to Süleyman's status, lies at the head of his tomb.

The white limestone façade of Şemsi Ahmet Paşa Mosque at Üsküdar contrasts with the brightly coloured boats on the Bosphorus.

lie in impressive mausoleums in the outer courtyard garden, and the great architect himself, Sinan, is buried in a modest tomb just a short distance away.

Üsküdar (Scutari) [Map: DY]

Fine mosques, fountains and public baths surround the ferry-landing of the Asiatic suburb of Üsküdar (traditionally known as Scutari), but two of the most attractive features lie on the hills immediately above the town. **Atik Valide Camii** (Mosque of the Valide Sultan) dominates the skyline, and is widely regarded as one of the most magnificent Ottoman monuments in Turkey. Once again, the architect Sinan can take credit for its construction, in 1583, towards the end of his prolific life. Less than 1km (0.6 miles) to the south lies the vast **graveyard of Karaca Ahmet**, with its ranks of venerable Ottoman turbaned tombstones, set amongst dark groves of cypresses.

ALONG THE BOSPHORUS★★

For centuries, travellers have extolled the beauties of the Bosphorus, with its grand waterside mansions and palaces, fine summer embassies, springtime forests ablaze with pink Judas Trees, ever turbulent waters, and its incomparable sunsets. Today, forested slopes have given way to rashes of villas, and busy roads follow much of the shoreline. Yet, despite the destruction wrought by man, the Bosphorus still has a unique allure, and should be on every visitor's itinerary.

The Bosphorus is the unique waterway that separates Europe from Asia, and links the Black Sea to the Sea of Marmara (which itself drains through the Dardanelles into the Aegean Sea, and ultimately the Mediterranean). Running for 30km (18.5 miles), it varies from 700m (2 300ft) to

Ferries at Eminönü wait to take visitors up the Bosphorus.

3.5km (2 miles) in width, and averages 60m (200ft) in depth. Its name comes from the words 'Bos For' – the Ox Ford – for here, according to legend, a two-timing Zeus turned his beloved Io (daughter of the first King of Argos) into a white heifer to protect her from his wife, Hera. Not to be outdone, Hera sent a gadfly to torment the luckless Io, who in a frenzied moment leapt over the strait.

The attractions of the Bosphorus can be seen by land or by sea, but perhaps the best way is to take a **ferry tour** from **Eminönü** (near the new Galata Bridge) to **Anadolu Kavağı**. Special sight-seeing ferries leave up to three times a day, and take nearly two hours each way, with a break of two hours to sample local fish specialities or to amble up to the fine Genoese castle, **Yoros Kalesi**, overlooking the straits.

Ordering a quick snack of grilled fish on the dockside.

The following attractions are the main sights along the waterway, listing the European side first (travelling from city to Black Sea) followed by the Asian sites (from Black Sea back to Eminönü). Remember, the ferry does not stop to allow you to visit most of these places, so you may want to make a return trip by car to explore further.

European Shore

The **Dolmabahçe Sarayı**★★ (Dolmabahçe Palace) lies in all its opulent splendour on the shoreline between Kabataş and Beşiktaş. Its impressive marble façade is best seen by boat. During the early 19C, the successive Ottoman sultans grew increasingly tired of the oriental atmosphere of the Topkapı Palace, and instead looked west for inspiration. In 1842, Sultan Abdül Mecit commissioned the famous Balyan family to

The lavish exterior of the 19C Dolmabahçe Palace, fomerly the sultan's residence then the presidential palace.

design a new palace at Dolmabahçe, and this remained the imperial residence into the dying days of the Ottoman Empire.

One of the remarkable rooms inside the Dolmabahçe Palace.

No expense was spared in its construction or decoration. The core of the palace is the monumental State Hall (or Throne Room), flanked on either side by two wings containing state rooms and royal apartments. In total, the building comprises 285 rooms, including 43 large salons, six Turkish baths, staff quarters, an infirmary with pharmacy, barracks, stables, aviary and two harems (separate complexes for the Sultan and princes).

The interior provides the setting for an extravagant – some might even say overdone – collection of art treasures. Most notable among the treasures are Bohemian crystal chandeliers (including a 4.5 tonne giant with 750 lamps, the world's largest), a staircase with Baccarat crystal balusters, an outstanding collection of paintings, vast Hereke carpets, and the fine painted ceiling of the Throne Room, with the central dome soaring 36m (118ft) above the floor. Whether you love or loathe this exuberant

The attractive baroque Mosque of Sultan Abdül Mecit I along the waterfront at Ortaköy.

style, the palace should not be missed.

At **Beşiktaş**, the **Deniz Müzesi** (Maritime Museum) displays a wide range of uniforms, models of naval vessels and maps associated with Turkish naval history. Notable exhibits include the imperial caiques (rowing barges) used by sultans from the 17C onwards, and an early 16C map of America by Turkish cartographer Piri Reis.

Between Beşiktaş and Ortaköy lies the **Çırağan Sarayı** (Çırağan Palace). Built during the reign of Sultan Abdül Aziz (completed 1874), the palace was gutted by fire in 1910, leaving little but a blackened shell. So it remained, until the 1980s, when it was flamboyantly – if not wholly faithfully – restored as a deluxe hotel (*see* p.99).

Ortaköy★ retains much of its charming village atmosphere, and has attracted artists and craftsmen. On Sundays, the maze of narrow streets come alive with market stalls. The square adjacent to the ferry landing and nearby streets are full of bars, cafés and restaurants, and the area makes a pleasant lunch or evening spot. Dominating the waterfront is the **Mecidiye Camii** (Mosque of Sultan Abdül Mecit I), one of the finer baroque mosques in the city (1855).

Looming over the village of Ortaköy is the **Atatürk (Boğaziçi) Köprüsü** (Bosphorus Bridge), which at 1074m (3 524ft) between towers was the fourth-longest suspension bridge at the time of its opening on 29 October 1973, the 50th anniversary of the founding of the Turkish Republic.

Bebek was a favourite retreat for sultans and paşas, and retains a good deal of its former charm. Lying at the foot of the densely wooded slopes is the splendid 19C Art Nouveau building of the former

A Turkish fish-seller.

The walls of the fortress of Rumeli Hisarı were completed in just four months.

Egyptian Embassy. It is the first of many summer embassy buildings that line the Bosphorus shores between Bebek and Sarıyer. Before the Turkish capital moved to Ankara, diplomatic staff would move *en masse* to these summer mansions, to avoid the stifling summers in the city.

On the hill immediately after Bebek, lies the **Boğaziçi Üniversitesi** (Bosphorus University), formerly the first Robert College. Founded by the American missionary Cyrus Hamlin during the Crimean War (the present buildings date from 1868-1871), this is the oldest American college outside the United States, and remains one of Turkey's foremost educational institutions.

Dominating the Bosphorus at this point is the monumental **fortress of Rumeli Hisarı★**, built by Sultan Mehmet II (the Conqueror) in 1452, opposite the smaller fortress of Anadolu Hisarı, to sever the supply of grain from the Black Sea to the Byzantine city. Mehmet charged his three chief vezirs with the task of building the three towers, while he retained for himself the job of building the intervening curtain walls and barbican. Aided by 1 000 masons and 2 000 workmen, the task was completed in under four months. A garrison of 400 janissaries was stationed here and formidable cannons trained on the straits. With the sinking of a Venetian ship (and the impaling of the surviving captain and crew), Constantinople was cut off, and the countdown to its conquest by Mehmet had begun. Today, in altogether more peaceful times, the castle is used as an open-air venue for concerts.

Lying immediately to the north of Rumeli Hisarı is the **Fatih Sultan Mehmet Köprüsü** (Bridge of Mehmet the Conqueror). At 1 090m (3 575ft), it was the fifth-longest in the world at its opening, in 1988. However, a third Bosphorus bridge is already planned.

The **Sadberk Hanım Müzesi** (Sadberk Hanım Museum), housed in a splendid 19C summer mansion in **Sarıyer**, is a fine small archaeological and ethnographic museum,

Waterside houses and fishing nets at the village of Anadolu Kavağı on the Asian side of the Bosphorus, near the entrance to the Black Sea.

founded in 1980 in memory of Sadberk Hanım, wife of Turkish businessman Vehbi Koç. It houses her lifetime collection of silver, porcelain, jewellery, furniture and embroidery.

Sarıyer and **Beykoz** (on the Asian side) mark the boundary of the **Upper Bosphorus**, still a remarkably wild and beautiful stretch of the straits. As a result of its strategic position at the head of the straits, the area has been under military control until very recently. Today, it is again possible to visit the tiny villages that lie in secluded coves, such as **Garipçe** and **Rumeli Feneri** (European shore), and **Anadolu Feneri** and **Poyraz** (Asian Shore), to experience some of the wild beauty of the Bosphorus of former times. At Garipçe, according to legend, **Jason and his Argonauts** chased away the evil harpies, winged monsters who every meal time swooped down from the heavens to eat the food of blind King Phineus, whilst at the mouth of the Bosphorus, Jason skilfully guided his ship through the dreaded Clashing Rocks.

Asian Shore

If your ferry stops at **Anadolu Kavağı**, do make the short walk up the steep hill to the huge Genoese **Yoros Kalesi** (Yoros Castle), dating from the 14C. The views in both directions along the Bosphorus are stunning.

Like the European side, the villages of the Asian shore south of Andadolu Kavağı have now coalesced and lost much of their original identity, but the overall scene is still beautiful and ever-fascinating. On passing under the second bridge again, the small bay of **Anadolu Hisarı** comes into view, set at the mouth of the two small streams often referred to as the **Sweet Waters of Asia** (the 'sweet waters' on the European side lay at the head of the Golden Horn). The **medieval fortress** here was built by Sultan Beyazit I around 1390, and was later rebuilt by Mehmet II in 1452, at the time when he was constructing the altogether more formidable fortress on the European shore. Beyond the castle lies the small **Palace of Küçüksu**, a small summer pavilion built in 1857 for Sultan Abdül Mecit I in the charming Ottoman rococo style.

Along much of the Bosphorus shores are splendid wooden waterside mansions, the **yalı**, built by the city's more prosperous citizens, some dating back to the late 17C. Whilst most remain in private hands and are therefore not open to the public, this is no hindrance as they are best viewed from the water. Some of the finest lie along the Asian shore around the two bridges, most notably **Amcazade Hüseyin Paşa Yalısı**, **Kıbrıslı Yalısı**, and the red **Kırmızı Yalı**.

Before finally returning to the ferry-landing, the village of **Beylerbeyi**, set at the foot of the first bridge, deserves a look; its cheap-and-cheerful fish restaurants on the promenade by the village's fine mosque are a good place to dine.

However, the principal attraction of the village is the **Beylerbeyi Sarayı★** (Beylerbeyi Palace), completed in 1865 by Sarkis Balyan, brother of the architect of the Dolmabahçe Palace. This sizeable palace is much smaller than the Dolmabahçe Palace, and in many ways is all the more attractive for it. It was restored and converted into a museum in the 1970s.

Wooden mansions along the Bosphorus at Emirğan.

EXCURSIONS FROM İSTANBUL

Visitors could spend months taking in all that İstanbul has to offer, but for those wishing to take a break from the city's hectic pace, the following places are worth a visit. Collectively, they would form an enjoyable 5-day tour, or you may prefer to pick just one or two to form the basis of a good weekend break. Private coaches serve all the towns mentioned, but the more intrepid may prefer to hire a car and take to the road.

Kızıl Adalar★ (Princes' Islands)

To get away from the hustle and bustle of the city for the day, take a ferry to the relative peace of the Princes' Islands, a cluster of nine small islands set in the Sea of Marmara south-east of the city.

Historically, the islands were a favoured retreat of monks and nuns who lived in a series of monasteries and convents. All too often, they were joined by deposed and exiled Byzantine emperors and empresses. Little remains of these religious establishments, although the **monastery of St George**, set on the highest hill on the island of Büyükada, makes an attractive excursion for visitors.

Instead, day-trippers come to view the fine wooden 19C mansions that grace the main islands, and to relax in the shade of pines, only interrupted by the gentle clop of horses' hooves, for cars are banned here. Ferries from Sirkeci leave daily and call at the four largest islands. Visitors will find most to interest them on the islands of **Büyükada** (Byzantine Prinkipo) and **Heybeliada** (Byzantine Halki), where horse-drawn phaetons can be hired on landing.

Goods are unloaded onto the waiting horses and carts at the harbour, Princes' Islands.

İznik★

Lying on fertile plains along the shore of İznik Lake, **İznik** is a sleepy agricultural town worthy of a half-day stopover. Its lakeside location and position on important southerly trade routes mean the town has attracted (and been conquered by) successive waves of invaders, including the Greeks, Romans, Byzantines, Arabs, Seljuk Turks and Ottomans. The town was founded in 316 BC by Alexander's general Antigonus, and the encircling **town walls** were built to defend the town after Alexander's death. Despite these walls, the town fell to **Lysimachus**, who renamed it **Nicaea** after his wife. The city was capital of Roman Bithynium in the 1C-3C, and flourished again in the Byzantine period. Consequently, the city boasts a wide range of

Roman, Byzantine and Ottoman buildings (although not all are in good repair).

Nicaea also played an important role in the history of Christianity; two important ecumenical councils were held here, leading to the **Nicaene Creed**, which remains the basis of Eastern Orthodox beliefs to this day, and the resolution of the Iconoclast controversy.

Renamed İznik in the 14C, the city made a lasting contribution to art and architecture with the beautiful **İznik tiles** and pottery which adorn so many great buildings to this day.

The most impressive structures are the double walls, largely rebuilt in Byzantine times, and including four principal gateways, most notably the northern **İstanbul Gate★**, which includes the remains of a triumphal arch built to honour the visit of Emperor Hadrian in AD 123. Look also for the **Roman amphitheatre** (2C) which has been partly excavated to reveal the structure, numerous Roman and later pottery and artefacts, and mosaics of charioteers. It is estimated that it could seat about 15 000 spectators. **Ayasofya Camii★** (Church of Haghia Sophia, built in 1065, on the site of a 6C church) and the **Yeşil Cami★** (Green Mosque, late 14C) are worth a visit. The **Archaeological Museum** has Roman finds, a well-preserved sarcophagus, and tiles from the old kilns.

Bursa★★

With its dramatic position at the foot of Uludağ, the Bithynian Mount Olympus, and set in fertile plains, 'green' Bursa has always been popular amongst Turks. Founded by Bithynian King Prusias I in 186 BC (hence the city's earlier names of Prusa, and later

Brusa), the city was the first capital of the Ottoman Empire from 1326 to 1361.

Today, the city is one of the most prosperous in Turkey, with a population of over 1 million. But be sure to press on through the outer industrial and residential suburbs: the old city is not only picturesque, but contains a wealth of early Ottoman buildings. Among the most famous are the **Ulu Cami**★ (Great Mosque, late 13C) with its pillared interior supporting 20 domes, and **Yeşil Cami**★★★ (Green Mosque, 1423), built in the typical Bursa-style with two domed halls, and decorated with fine green tiles. The adjacent **Yeşil Türbe**★★ (Green Tomb), also clad in green tiles, is the final resting place of Sultan Mehmet I. The **Muradiye**★, built between 1424 and 1426 by Murat II, was the last imperial mosque complex to be built in Bursa. It comprises the mosque, a *medrese* (college), an *imaret* (dispensing free food for the poor) and the tomb of Murat II.

The twenty domes of Ulu Cami, Bursa, are supported by twelve freestanding pillars.

Bursa is an excellent place to purchase silks.

Bursa's important role in the **silk** industry is best represented in the **Koza Han**★ (silk bazaar or silk-cocoon hall). Entirely occupied by silk merchants, it is a magnificent place to wander, recently renovated and with ample opportunites to stop for refreshing tea. If you visit in late June or early July, you may be lucky enough to see the cocoon auction, where local breeders from the province gather to sell their produce.

Uludağ★, at 2 543m (8 343ft), is reached by cable car or public *dolmuş* from Bursa, and is worth visiting at any time of the year. During the summer, the forests and alpine pastures provide excellent hiking – look out for brown bear and the 25 or so wild plants found nowhere else. In winter, it is transformed into Turkey's largest ski resort, served by 15 hotels (although very expensive). The mountain was declared a National Park in 1961.

Finally, after a brisk day's hiking or skiing, visit the suburb of **Çekirge** (west of the main town) for a thermal bath. A number of historic baths still function (notably the 16C **Yeni Kaplıca**), while most of the larger hotels have copious steaming water straight from the heart of the mountain.

Troy★

About 200km (124 miles) west of Bursa lies the **Dardanelles** (Çanakkale Boğazı), the straits separating the Sea of Marmara from the Aegean. Some 30km (18.6 miles) to the south is the site of **Troy**. Here, according to Homeric tradition, a decade-long war between the Greeks and Trojans was fought, following the kidnapping of beautiful Helen (wife of Menelaus, King of Sparta) by Paris

A modern reconstruction of the fabled horse of Troy stands near the house that Schliemann lived in while carrying out his excavations.

(son of Trojan King Priam). Archaeologists have long disputed the exact location of Troy, or, indeed, whether the events recounted in Homer's *Iliad* ever took place at all. Substantive proof was ultimately provided by the German entrepreneur and amateur archaeologist, Heinrich Schliemann, whose own story is as exciting as the story of Troy itself. From 1868, Schliemann excavated the site, making the momentous discovery of 'King Priam's Gold' in 1873. The gold – smuggled out of Turkey very much against the wishes of the Ottoman government – probably pre-dates Homer's Troy by perhaps 1 000 years, but Schliemann can take credit for establishing Troy's true identity.

While natural disaster and war have conspired to reduce Troy's buildings to rubble, this archaeological site is of exceptional historic importance, with its nine cities superimposed upon one another, chronicling 5 000 years of occupation. For the visitor, the mound at **Hisarlık**, overlooking the flat marshlands stretching to the Aegean, nevertheless presents an evocative picture, steeped in history.

Çanakkale⋆

A crossing of the Dardanelles at Çanakkale (the best base for touring the area) brings the visitor back into Europe and onto the Gelibolu Peninsula, best known for the bitter battles fought during the **Gallipoli campaign** of the First World War. In 1915, Britain organised a naval assault of the straits as a prelude to capturing the Ottoman capital itself (Turkey had allied itself with the Germans). During the following nine months, British, French, Australian, New Zealand and Indian forces fought Turks in bitter trench warfare, before finally retreating. A young Turkish officer, Lieutenant-Colonel **Mustafa Kemal**, distinguished himself during the bloody campaign. Later he was destined to become Atatürk, 'father' and president of the newly-founded Turkish Republic. Peaceful forests of pine clothe much of the peninsula where

Memorials at the battlefields of Gallipoli.

there were once battlegrounds, but the extensive cemeteries and monuments to the war dead are poignant reminders of the human cost of this most terrible of campaigns.

Edirne★

Lying at the current frontier zone with Greece and Bulgaria, Edirne (formerly Adrianople) remains an important strategic settlement on the main trade routes west. Despite recent industrial prosperity, the town still retains much of the charms of an old Turkish town, and is well worth a full day's sightseeing. With its capture by Sultan Murat I, Edirne became the second capital of the Ottoman Empire until the conquest of Constantinople in 1453. As a result, the town is effectively an open-air museum of early Ottoman architecture.

Notable amongst the many buildings are the **Eski Cami★** (Old Mosque, 1414), built in the multi-domed Bursa Ulu Cami style; the **Üç Serefeli Camii★** (Mosque of Three Balconies, 15C), transitional between the Bursa and Classical styles; and the **Beyazit II Camii★★** (Mosque of Beyazit II, 1488). However, pride of place must go to Sinan's **Selimiye Camii★★★** (Mosque of Selim II), built in 1574 towards the end of the great Ottoman architect's life, and justly regarded as one of his greatest masterpieces for its exceptional use of space and light. Edirne's other main claim to fame is as the home of **grease wrestling**, when brawny Turkish men pit their strength against one another, clad in leather breeches and drenched in olive oil. The annual contests take place in the **Kırkpınar Stadium**, situated in attractive riverside meadows below the town, during June and July.

Turkish Baths

A visit to a Turkish bath or 'hamam' is one of the most relaxing and pleasurable experiences of a trip to İstanbul, yet most visitors leave without indulging!

In the age before bathrooms in private homes, hamams were not only a place to bathe, but also an important social and recreational centre. Here İstanbulites came to wash, benefit from the healing powers of the waters (said to free the body of toxins, to cleanse the pores, and to cure all sorts of ills, from scabies to impotence), as well to chat and sip tea.

Many of the finest baths date from the golden age of the Ottoman Empire, often built as part of the larger mosque complexes, to serve the local population and to generate revenue for the upkeep of the mosque. A typical hamam has three sections: a large domed derobing room (*camekan*), a cool section (*soğukluk*) and the hot room (*hararet*). The latter is generally cruciform in plan, with a central large marble slab heated from below (*göbek taşı*) on which the customers lie to sweat and be massaged, before moving to one of the washing basins around the walls of the chamber for a vigorous scrub-down. Needless to say, men and women are segregated either in separate sections of the baths (in larger double hamams), or by bathing on different days.

So next time you pass a Turkish hamam, pluck up courage and take the plunge. If you choose one of the tourist-oriented baths, the staff will show you what to do, so all you have to do is to enjoy the atmosphere and simply relax.

Selected Hamams

Cağaloğlu Hamamı (Prof. Kazım Gürkan Caddesi 34) Perhaps the most important architecturally, it was commissioned by Sultan Mahmut I (1741), and used by Florence Nightingale, Franz Liszt and Edward VIII. Expensive.

Çemberlitaş Hamamı (Vezirhan Caddesi 8) Situated next to the Constantine Arch, from which it gets its name (built c.1583).

Galatasaray Hamamı (Turnacıbaşı Sokak 2, Beyoğlu) Built as part of the Galata Palace at the end of the 18C.

These are the three most popular hamams used by tourists, but for braver visitors some of the other classical Ottoman hamams – often tucked away down side streets – offer a unique experience.

The Cağaloğlu Hamamı.

WEATHER

The summer season in İstanbul runs from mid-June to mid-September. July and August are the hottest months, with daytime temperatures reaching 30°C (86°F) which, combined with relatively high humidity, can make sightseeing uncomfortable. May/June and September/early October are the best times to visit, though if you are unlucky the autumn rains may set in during October. Although hot during the day, cooling breezes from the Bosphorus make the evenings cooler, so pack a sweater or jacket.

Most rain falls between November and March (annual total about 70cm/27.5ins), when the temperature is cool rather than cold. Snow does fall in the city – typically a smattering on higher ground which lasts for only a day or two.

Finally, if you arrive and the weather is

poor, do not despair. The common belief amongst locals is that İstanbul weather rarely stays the same for more than three days in a row, and the sun shines brightly for more than half the days of the year.

CALENDAR OF EVENTS

Throughout the year, the city is host to an increasingly wide range of festivals, performances and exhibitions, in addition to the national public holidays (marked by an asterisk).

1 January* New Year's Day – despite the city's predominately Muslim faith, this is a time for giving cards and presents, and you will see the occasional 'Christmas' tree.

April İstanbul International Film Festival.

23 April* National Sovereignty Day (also termed Children's Day) – marking the anniversary of the first meeting of the Grand National Assembly.

May-September Sound and light displays outside the Blue Mosque.

Mid-May to mid-June International Yapı Kredi Youth Festival.

19 May* Youth Day – commemorating Atatürk's birthday.

June-July Traditional grease wrestling competitions at Kırkpınar Stadium, Edirne.

Mid-June to mid-July İstanbul International Music Festival.

July Folklore and Music Festival in Bursa, one of Turkey's best folk-dancing festivals.

July İstanbul International Jazz Festival.

30 August* Victory Day – commemorating the victory of Republican Turks over the Greeks at Dumlupınar, during the Turkish War of Independence in 1922.

29 October* Republic Day – celebrating the birth of the Turkish Republic in 1923.

In addition to these public holidays, there are a number of religious festivals which are celebrated according to the Hicri (Muslim lunar calendar). As this is about 11 days shorter than the western Gregorian calendar, the festivals take place nearly a fortnight earlier in every successive year. Two are particularly significant, and may affect visitors' plans:

Şeker Bayramı (Feast of Sugar, also called Ramazan Bayramı in Turkish, Ramadan in English) is a three-day holiday to mark the end of the month of day-time fasting. (Food is available in tourist areas in the city during the month of fast, but it is polite to be discreet when eating, when others are fasting.)

Kurban Bayramı (Feast of the Sacrifice, 2 months 10 days after Ramadan) The most important public holiday of the year, this four-day holiday commemorates the devotion of Abraham. To test his loyalties, God ordered Abraham to sacrifice his son, Isaac. Only moments before Abraham performed the deed, God intervened, praising Abraham, and ordering him to sacrifice a ram in Isaac's place. According to tradition, over 2 million rams are slaughtered across Turkey during the festival, many within the city.

During these festivals the roads out of the city may be gridlocked, and shops closed, so plan accordingly.

ACCOMMODATION

Accommodation in İstanbul is not typical of Turkey. At the top end of the scale are the luxury modern international hotels with every amenity. As an alternative to these very comfortable but rather impersonal establishments are the older, imperial-style hotels in Beyoğlu built towards the end of

Ritual washing before prayer at an İstanbul mosque.

the 19C. These have great elegance and character, and give a better flavour of the city.

Further down the price scale are the mid-range modern hotels where standards are adequate. Best value of all, are the converted Ottoman houses in the heart of old İstanbul.

There is a good choice of *pansiyons* (pensions). Offering good value and often a genuine experience of the city, they are simply furnished and fairly basic; ask to see the room before you agree to take it. Students with internationally recognised cards can stay at Turkish Youth hostels.

Hotels registered with the Ministry of Tourism are known as 'touristic hotels' and have a 1- to 5-star rating; this does not really equate with the European system, but it gives some idea of what to expect (note that not all good hotels choose to be registered).

A guide to prices, per double room per night, is as follows (as inflation is high, prices are quoted in $ US): 5-star: $175-225; 4-star: $85-180; 3-star: $65-85; 2-star: $40-70; 1-star: under $40.

Hotel Recommendations

It is well worth selecting hotels for their location and atmosphere. Among the most popular are the deluxe **Çırağan Palace Hotel** (Çırağan Cad. 84; ☎ 212 258 3377), an opulent sultan's palace, situated on the shores of the Bosphorus. However, it may well be beyond the pocket of many travellers (around $220 per night). Older, far less luxurious and less expensive (around $105 per night) the **Pera Palas Hotel** (Meşrutiyet Cad. 98-100; ☎ 212 251 4560) was built to serve travellers using the *Orient Express* and was a favourite with the likes of Atatürk and Agatha Christie (she wrote *Murder on the Orient Express* here). Worth visiting, if only to have a coffee and experience the sheer luxury and charm of the surroundings.

The newly-opened **Four Seasons Hotel**

The elegant exterior of the Çırağan Palace Hotel.

(Tevkifhane Sokak No 1, Sultanahmet; ☎ 212 638 8200) occupies the beautifully converted historic Sultanahmet Prison. (expensive, ranging from $225-295).

The **Yeşil Ev Hotel** (Kabasakal Cad. 5; ☎ 212 517 6785) handily situated in Sultanahmet, and the **Kariye Hotel** (Kariye Camii Sok. 18, Edirnekapi; ☎ 212 534 8414), adjacent to the small yet exquisite Kariye Camii, some distance from the city's historic centre, are charming old converted Ottoman homes. Although less luxurious than the city's best, they have an intimate charm of their own. There is also the hotel **Ayasofia Evleri** (Sogukçesme Sok ☎ 513 36 60), near Ayasofya and the Topkapı Palace. This complex of nine old wooden houses with pastel façades boasts a restaurant sited in an old byzantine cistern. **L'Obelisk** (Amiral Tadfil ☎ 517 71 73) is a charming old, converted Ottoman house with a restaurant decorated in pure Ottoman style, situated in the Sultanahmet region. In the same area, is **L'Amber** (☎ 518 81 19). Austere façade, but this 19C hotel provides all modern comforts. **Avicenna** hotel (Amiral Tafdil, Sultanahmet ☎ 517 05 50) is quiet and comfortable.

For moderate to inexpensive hotels, look around the Sultanahmet, the Laleli district of the old town and the Taksim area. Try the **Büyük Londra** (Meşrutiyet Caddesi 117, Beyoğlu ☎ 212 149 1925) in the Taksim district, near the famous Pera Palas, it shares some of the latter's 19C chandeliered charm.

FOOD AND DRINK

One of the finer legacies of the Ottoman Empire is Turkish cuisine. *Şiş kebap* (shish kebab), stuffed vine leaves cooked in olive oil, and *baklava* are amongst the classic dishes known by lovers of fine food the world over.

Turkish **breakfast** is a simple yet wholesome affair: *beyaz peynir* (white cheese), olives, jams and mounds of fresh crusty bread, served with Turkish tea. However, increasingly the hotels catering for tourists offer wider fare, including cereal, yoghurt, juices and so on.

A typical **lunch** (usually served between noon and 2pm) might be taken at a *kebabçı*

A tempting display of fish and seafood outside a restaurant in Anadolu Kavağı.

or *köfteci*, serving a range of kebabs and minced-meat dishes. Among the most popular kebabs are *Şiş kebap*, skewers of succulent cubes of lamb (or chicken), with a sprinkle of salt, barbecued, and *döner kebap*, layered lamb on a revolving spit, sliced as the outer layer becomes cooked. A popular kebab using döner meat is the *İskender kebabçı*, döner meat over a bed of grilled *pide* bread, and served with yoghurt, a rich tomato sauce and topped with piping hot browned butter – delicious, if fattening!

However, Turks reserve the evening for big meals, at a good *lokanta* (restaurant) or *meyhane* (tavern). The **evening meal** might start with a range of *meze* – cold and hot hors-d'ouevres. There are many types of *meze*, but particularly popular are fresh vegetables cooked in olive oil, *haydari* (yoghurt with garlic and dill), *çerkez tavuğu* (a purée of chicken and walnuts), and a range of hot *börek* (tasty cheese or meat in wafer-thin filo pastry, deep fried or baked). You can also taste *cacik* (a cold soup with garlic, yogurt and chopped cucmber), *çig köfte* (raw, spicy meatballs), *pilaki* (a mixture of French beans, herbs and onions browned in olive oil and tomato), *peynir* (cheese from ewe's and cow's milk), *lakerda* (marinated fish), *midye tavasi* (mussel fritters), *tarama* (a dish made from grey mullet's eggs, lemon and oil) and *patlican salatasi* (aubergine salad). Look out for *imam bayıldı* ('fainting imam'), another aubergine dish so delicious you may swoon like the legendary imam. The waiter will typically bring a tray of different *mezes*, which are shared by the whole table.

For many, the *mezes* will be a meal in themselves, but others will choose to follow them with further courses. **Fish** and grilled **meats** are particularly popular, and some restaurants will offer a range of hot dishes, such as casseroles. Except in the smartest restaurants, there may be no menus on the table. Instead, the waiter will be happy to take you to the kitchen to show what is on offer that evening. You can choose from a range of steaming pans, or select the meat or fish which looks most tempting. It is worth remembering that the widest range of fish is available in the autumn and winter months, when they are caught during their passage through the Bosphorus.

Sweet delacacies are rarely eaten after a meal. The Turks prefer to savour them with **afternoon tea**. Pastries made of honey, almonds and cream delight the palates of goumets! Be tempted by *kadayif* (a sort of vermicelli grilled with honey, almonds and sesame), *diber dudagi* 'beautiful lips', (walnuts,

almonds, honey and rose water), *revani* (cream baba), *hanim göbegi* 'woman's navel' (a fritter filled with sweetened cream), *firin sütlaç* (rice pudding), the delicious but very sweet *baklava* (wafer thin layers of pastry, steeped in honey or syrup, and stuffed with walnuts or pistachios), or pears and quince, served with *kaymak* (thick cream). The most adventurous should try *tavuk gögüsü*, a pudding made of milk, sugar and minced chicken breast.

A Turkish meal would not be complete without a cup of **Turkish coffee**. Made by bringing coffee grounds and water to the boil three times, with sugar added at this stage. Ask for *sade* (unsweetened), *orta* (medium sweet) or *şekerli* (very sweet). **Tea** (*çay*), the other national drink, comes from

Eating out in a restaurant in Ortaköy Square.

the Rize region. It is brewed for a long time, then served in small glasses with lots of sugar. Turks often drink tea during the day, and offer it as a gesture of welcome to guests. Apple-flavoured tea has just come onto the market.

As Muslims, Turks are not great drinkers of alcohol, but they do make an exception for *rakı*, the national aniseed-based alcoholic beverage typically served with water. **Wines** are gaining in popularity, and the winehouses of Kavaklıdere (Ankara) and Doluca (Mürefte) are producing some excellent wines in sufficient variety to suit most tastes. **Beer** is usually sold bottled (canned varieties are available, but are more expensive). Try the Turkish brews: Efes Pilsen, Tuborg and Venus.

A traditional sherbet- or lemonade-seller.

Restaurant Recommendations

For a simple meal of *mezes* and grilled meats or fish, the *meyhanes* (taverns) situated in and around **Ortaköy Square**, bathed in a gentle breeze off the Bosphorus, or those along **Nevizade Sokak** (the first street off right from Beyoğlu's colourful Balık Pazari), are lively and ever-popular. You can dine out in typically Turkish restaurants, such as the **Darüzziyafe**, Sifahane Caddesi 6 ☎ 511 84 14, near the Mosque of Süleyman the Magnificent, where the cuisine is excellent and the setting charming. In summer it is possible to eat in an inner courtyard. The **Haci Baba**, Istiklal Caddesi 49, ☎ 244 18 86, serves meze and other Turkish fare, all displayed in the window to assist with choice. The **Beyti,** Orman Sokak 33, ☎ 573 92 12, a restaurant of the Ottoman period, looks on to the Marmara Sea. Grilled mutton and beef are its specialities. The restaurant

Urcan, Orta Cesme Cad. 2/1 ☎ 242 03 67 specialises in delicious, specially prepared fish dishes at prices to match. The **Galata Kulesi** ☎ 245 11 60, is situated at the top of the Galata Tower. Take advantage of the outstanding view over İstanbul by having lunch here.

Some of the finest traditional Ottoman cuisine is to be found in the large hotels. Among the best are the **Çırağan**, **Conrad** and **Swissôtel** hotels, all overlooking the Bosphorus.

SHOPPING

İstanbul is a shopper's paradise, with goods – old and new – to suit all tastes. **Bargaining** is very much a way of life here, particularly in the bazaars (though not in the new

A carpet-seller displaying his wares.

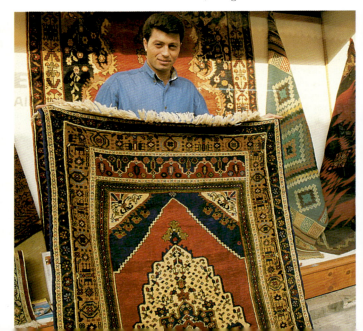

shopping malls), so be prepared to bargain hard. It can be fun! Ask the seller his starting price, and make a counter-offer (perhaps as little as 50 per cent), and carry on making counter-offers until a price is agreed. Do not be intimidated by the shopkeeper's sales talk, nor feel obliged because you have drunk one too many cups of free tea. However, if you do start bargaining, you should be prepared to buy the item if the seller agrees to your price.

There are few better places to buy **oriental carpets** than İstanbul, with a vast selection from all across Turkey, as well as the Caucasus, Iran and central Asia. Good carpets are made of pure wool, wool with cotton, or (most expensive) silk, and come in three basic styles: *halı* (pile rugs and carpets), *kilims* (flat-weave carpets) and *sumak* (embroidered). Rug-selecting is an art. For pile carpets, the knots on the underside should be tight and even (count the number per square centimetre for a guide). Natural dyes are popular, but check that these are colour-fast, whether darker colours have run onto lighter tones. Finally, avoid synthetic fibres, which do not last long. The widest range of carpet shops are in and around the Grand Bazaar and Arasta Bazaar (below the Blue Mosque), and along Nuruosmaniye Caddesi.

For **antiques** visit the Çukurcuma area (below İstiklal Caddesi, Beyoğlu), where shops sell virtually anything old, at a price. For those with limited budgets, the *bit pazarı* (flea markets) scattered across the city offer better bargains. But remember, the export of antiques from Turkey without written permission is forbidden, and customs officers regard the matter very seriously.

Colourful Turkish slippers are a popular souvenir.

Spices for sale in the Egyptian Bazaar.

Copper and brassware make attractive souvenirs. Being durable, large quantities of late-Ottoman copperware is available at fair prices, from plates and ladles to henna jars and egg poachers. The Old Bedesten, at the heart of the Grand Bazaar, and the flea markets have the best selection.

With cheap labour, **gold** represents good value. Serious buyers should check out the daily price of unworked gold posted in the Kuyumcular Caddesi (the Street of the Jewellers), in the Grand Bazaar, as a guide before buying. The Grand Bazaar and the Egyptian Bazaar are the best areas. **Onyx** is mined in Cappadocia and from it jewellery, vases, chess sets etc. are made. The quality of the stone depends on its colour. Green with brown veins is rare, whilst brown-veined beige is the most common and veined white and plain colours are not considered good quality. The price depends on the colour and cut of the object.

Pipes in **sea foam** are a Turkish speciality as are **narghiles** (pipe and water-bottle apparatus, through which smoke is drawn into the mouth). These may be decorated with precious stones and golden arabesques or simply coloured glass. The miniature ones make excellent souvenirs.

There is a mouth-watering selection of **spices and foodstuffs** on offer, particularly from the Egyptian (Spice) Bazaar. The range is limitless, but most popular are the spices, a variety of herbal teas, Turkish Delight and marzipan, caviar, and dried fruits and nuts.

Leather and suede is big business in Turkey, and can be very good value for money, given that the buyer is careful to check the quality of the leather itself and the workmanship. Leather merchants are found in and around the Grand Bazaar, and up-market brands can be found in the shopping malls.

High fashion has come to İstanbul in a big way, offering everything from designer jeans (beware of fakes) to the very best from the world's famous fashion labels (including a number of comparably good Turkish fashion houses). Quality is uniformly good and affordable, particularly during the January and July *indirim* (sales). Socialites shop at a series of glitzy new shopping malls, as well as in the more traditional fashion districts of town at Nişantaşı and Beyoğlu.

Shopping Recommendations

For the sheer experience, the old bazaars of the market quarter offer some of the best, and most enjoyable, shopping opportunities. The **Egyptian** or **Spice Bazaar** has the best

range of traditionally oriental foodstuffs and spices, whilst the **Grand Bazaar** offers much else, from leather jackets to carpets, and old copperware to handsome ceramics (*see* p.106). However, it is in the intervening streets between these two bazaars that many of the city's inhabitants do their shopping. In this veritable labyrinth of streets, tiny shops are packed to bursting.

For those whose shopping tastes are more sedate and European, many large new shopping malls have opened in recent years in the city's smarter suburbs. The best on offer at present is **Akmerkez**, in Etiler, winner of both the International Council of Shopping Centres' Best Shopping Centre of Europe Award 1995, and the 1996 International Design and Development Award. A shuttle bus service is available from the larger hotels.

ENTERTAINMENT AND NIGHTLIFE

In a city as large and cosmopolitan as İstanbul, there is something to suit all tastes. For details, check the press or one of the (bi)monthly magazine guides to the city.

Performing Arts

İstanbul is gaining a well-deserved reputation for its increasingly varied range of opera, ballet, concerts and recitals, which take place in the **Atatürk Cultural Centre** (AKM) in Taksim Square, and in the 30 additional municipal and privately-run theatres. Particularly popular are the performances that take place in historic buildings and open-air venues around the city, most notably in the Byzantine church of **Aya İrini** (otherwise closed to the public), and within the castle walls of **Yediküle** (on the Theodosian Land Walls, adjacent to the Sea of Marmara) and **Rumeli Hisarı**, Mehmet the Conqueror's monumental fortification along the Bosphorus.

The highlight of the musical year is the **İstanbul International Music Festival**, an annual extravaganza taking place in June and July, since 1973. This typically features a wide range of orchestral concerts, chamber music, recitals, opera, dance, and traditional Turkish folkloric performances. Undoubtedly the most popular attraction of the festival is the annual performance of Mozart's opera *Abduction from the Seraglio*, performed, appropriately, within the grounds of the Topkapı Palace. Early booking is essential.

Bars and Nightclubs

Nightclubs are a growth industry in the city. They range from the somewhat sleazy to the ultra-smart, frequented by İstanbul's *nouveau riche*. All have bars, and many offer food, discos, live music, and occasionally floor

The busy İstiklal Caddesi has many nightclubs, cinemas and boutiques.

shows (including belly dancing, though this is not popular amongst locals). The clubs are mainly around Taksim and Beyoğlu, Etiler, along the European shores of the Bosphorus between Ortaköy and Bebek, and along Bağdat Caddesi (situated in Asian İstanbul). A word of warning: do not be lured into one of the sleazy *gazinos* (bars with floor show and 'hostesses') situated in the side streets off İstiklal Caddesi, or you may find yourself barred from leaving until you have settled an outrageous bill.

Bosphorus Cruises

A very pleasant way to spend an evening is to take a cruise up the Bosphorus, which has a magical appearance after dark. Perhaps the best cruises are offered by the larger hotels (notably the Swissôtel and Conrad), and the tour price usually includes a buffet supper.

The skyline of the Golden Horn is unforgettable in the evening light.

SPORTS

Football is *the* national sport of Turkey. After any major match, the city's main thoroughfares are choked with supporters, chanting, honking horns, and waving flags from car windows, often well into the early hours of the morning. Yet Turkish supporters treat foreign spectators with remarkable good humour. İstanbul has three professional teams – Beşiktaş, Fenerbahçe and Galatasaray – which play their home games in stadiums in Beşiktaş, Şişli and Kızıltoprak respectively.

Swimming has always been popular with Istanbulites; on sunny summer Sundays crowds head north to the Black Sea or to the beaches of the Princes' Islands, to picnic and swim. The Black Sea season is shorter than that of the Mediterranean, and is at its best between June and September. Slightly lower temperatures and mild saltiness make it delightfully refreshing. The best beaches are at Kilyos, on the European side of the Bosphorus (25km/15.5 miles north of the city), and west of Şile, on the Asian side (70km/44 miles north-east).

All the luxury hotels have modern **health clubs** as well as swimming pools. Most allow non-residents to use these facilities (at a price) on a daily or weekly basis.

For those in search of greener surroundings, an increasing number of country clubs have been built out-of-town. These offer **horse riding** and **golfing** opportunities for visitors. Kemer Country, adjacent to the magnificent Long Aqueduct of Kemerburgaz (north of the city), and Klassis Hotel, Golf and Country Club at Silivri (west of the city), are now operational.

111

THE BASICS

Before You Go

For a stay of up to three months, citizens of Australia, Canada and New Zealand do not need a visa to enter Turkey. Travellers from Britain, Ireland and the US, however, do require a visa, which can be obtained on entry into the country. Full passports are generally required, although all EU citizens may enter with the requisite identity cards instead of a passport.

If you wish to take a car into Turkey for longer than three months, contact the Turkish Touring and Automobile Club, Halaskargazi Caddesi 364, Şişli, İstanbul ☎ (212) 231 4631. *See* **Driving** for the documents required.

No vaccinations are required by law, but it is recommended that vaccinations for polio, tetanus, typhoid and hepatitis-A are kept up to date.

Getting There

The vast majority of people travelling to Turkey do so by air and Turkish Airlines (THY), as well as other international airlines, operate regular flights to İstanbul from the principal cities of the world. İstanbul's airport, Atatürk, is 25km (16 miles) to the west of the city at Yeşilköy ☎ (212) 663 6363. THY has offices all over the world, including Australia, Ireland, the UK and the US. On arrival at İstanbul's airport you can take one of the THY buses into the city, which is the cheapest way. The Havas buses run half-hourly to Beyoğlu via Şişhane (near Taksim Square). Alternatively, you can take a taxi, which are reasonably priced and more convenient. The journey takes about 30 minutes.

By rail, İstanbul can be reached directly from some of the major cities in Europe. In

view of the ongoing troubles in Yugoslavia, it is advisable to opt for one of the safe routes through Austria, Hungary, Romania and Bulgaria. Information is available from Turkish Railways (TCDD) ☎ (212) 527 0050/1 and travel agents in your own country. Reservations can also be made on ☎ (212) 249 9222.

It is possible to drive to İstanbul from Europe either by taking a route through Romania and Bulgaria, or heading for Italy then boarding a ferry to Turkey. To give you an idea of the distances involved, London to İstanbul is about 3 000km (1 875 miles).

For information about all car ferries to Turkey – other possibilities are from Northern Cypress and the Greek Islands – contact Turkish Maritime Lines (TML) Rıhtım Caddesi, Karaköy, İstanbul ☎ (212) 244 0207 or, before you leave, try the Tourist Information Office in your home country.

Regular coach services operate between İstanbul and several European countries, as well as from Iraq, Iran and Saudi Arabia to the south.

Bus station at Eminönü.

Accidents and Breakdowns

If you are in a hired car, the rental firm should be able to help with breakdowns, so carry their details with you at all times. In the event of a breakdown in your own car, contact the Turkish Touring and Automobile Club for assistance: General Directorate, Oto Sanayı Sitesi Yanı 4, Levent ☎ (212) 282 8140.

Should you be involved in an accident, the traffic police ☎154 or the Gendarme ☎ 156 must be notified and will inform you of the subsequent procedure. You should not move your vehicle until the traffic police have arrived and written a report (of which you should keep a copy).

Accommodation *see* p.96

Airports *see* **Getting There**

Babysitters *see* **Children**

Banks

Banks are open from 8.30/9am-noon and 1.30-5pm, Monday to Friday. In tourist areas they are open every day. Most banks exchange foreign currency, although not necessarily at the best rate. *See also* **Money**

Beaches

If you want a break from the heat and bustle of the city, the Princes' Islands in the Sea of Marmara offer some reasonably-sized beaches. Ferry boats regularly ply to and fro on both the European and Asian shores of İstanbul. On the European side of the Black Sea, 25km (16 miles) from the edge of the city, are the long sandy beaches of Kilyos, while Şile on the Asian side of the Black Sea is 70km (44 miles) away.

Nudity on beaches is against the law, and would be wholly inappropriate on İstanbul beaches.

Bicycles

Cycling in İstanbul is not recommended, but if you are determined, your hotel should be able to suggest a hire shop.

Books

John Julius Norwich *The Byzantine Trilogy* (eminently readable history of Byzantium) Cyril Mango *Byzantium: the Empire of the New Rome* (authoritative history of Byzantium) Godfrey Goodwin *A History of Ottoman Architecture* (perhaps the best overview of the legacy of Ottoman architecture) Laurence Kelly *Istanbul: a Travellers' Companion* (a compendium of accounts and diaries of travellers to the city over the centuries) Agatha Christie *Murder on the Orient Express* Apollonius of Rhodes *Jason and the Argonauts* T Eliot *Diary of an Idle Woman in Constantinople*

Breakdowns see Accidents

Buses see Transport

Camping

There are about 40 camp sites in the Marmara region, some of which are within easy reach of İstanbul. Most have good facilities, including a restaurant, and some have private beaches. They are usually closed from October to April. The Turkish camping organisation is Türkiye Kamp ve Karavan Derneği, Nenehatun Caddesi 96, Gaziosmanpaşa, Ankara ☎ (312) 436 3151.

Car Hire

Most international car hire firms are represented in İstanbul, but unless you are going to travel out of the city it is far better to rely on taxis, which are cheap and plentiful. You should avoid small private hire companies. Automatic cars are not usually available, and you should check

An İstanbul taxi.

beforehand with the hire company if an automatic drive car is required.

Drivers must be over 21 and have held a full driving licence for at least a year. Third party insurance is the minimum legal requirement, but it is advisable to take out collision damage waiver and personal accident insurance. Always check the tyres (including the spare), horn and brakes before setting off and make sure you know the procedure for summoning help if needs be.

Children
Turkish people love children and welcome them wherever they go. There is plenty that will appeal to them in İstanbul and there are also many parks and open spaces. Some hotels offer a babysitting service; ask at reception. Children travel on public transport at reduced fares.

Pharmacies stock nappies and baby foods, although the brand names may not be familiar and jars of baby food may be hard to come by.

Climate *see p.94*

Clothing
Light, cotton clothing and flat, comfortable shoes (easily removed for visits to mosques)

should form the basis of your wardrobe. The evenings can be chilly in comparison to the heat of the day, so a sweater or two is advisable. When visiting mosques, women should cover their hair so a headscarf is useful.

Most Turkish shoe and clothes sizes follow the standard current throughout Europe, but differ from those in the UK and US. The following are examples:

Dress Sizes

UK	8	10	12	14	16	18
Europe	38	40	42	44	46	48
US	6	8	10	12	14	16

Men's Suits

UK & US	36	38	40	42	44	46
Europe	46	48	50	52	54	56

Men's Shirts

UK & US	14.5	15	15.5	16	16.5	17
Europe	37	38	39/40	41	42	43

Men's Shoes

UK	7	7.5	8.5	9.5	10.5	11
Europe	41	42	43	44	45	46
US	8	8.5	9.5	10.5	11.5	12

Women's Shoes

UK	4.5	5	5.5	6	6.5	7
Europe	38	38	39	39	40	41
US	6	6.5	7	7.5	8	8.5

Complaints
If any complaints cannot be satisfactorily resolved on the spot with the person in charge, the Tourist Information Office may be able to advise you,

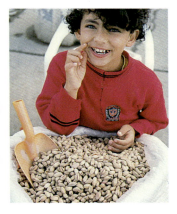

depending on the nature of the problem.

Consulates

Consulates can be found at the following addresses:

Australia Tepecik Yolu Sokak, No 58 Etiler ☎ (212) 257 7050
Canada Büyükdere Caddesi, Begüm Han, No 107/3 Gayrettepe ☎ (212) 272 5174
UK Meşrutiyet Caddesi No 34, Tepebaşı/Beyoğlu
☎ (212) 293 7540
US Meşrutiyet Caddesi No 104–108, Tepebaşı
☎ (212) 251 3602
Eire (Honorary Consulate), Cumhuriyet Caddesi No 26, Harbiye
☎ (212) 246 6025.

Crime

Violent crime is rare in İstanbul, but, as in any city, sensible precautions should be taken.

• Carry as little money, and as few credit cards, as possible, and leave any valuables in the hotel safe.
• Carry wallets and purses in secure pockets, wear body belts, or carry handbags across your body or firmly under your arm.
• Cars can be a target for opportunists, so never leave your car unlocked, and hide away or, better still, remove items of value.
• Beware of drug trafficking and never accept or agree to carry packages from strangers. Bags should never be left unattended, particularly at airports. *See also* **Emergencies**

Customs and Entry Regulations

Personal effects may be freely taken into Turkey but there is a limit of 200 cigarettes (or 50 cigars/200gm tobacco) and five litres of wine and/or spirits. Additional cigarettes and tobacco can be purchased from Turkish Duty Free shops on entering the country. Any antiques or valuable possessions being taken into the country must be registered in the owner's passport to avoid problems when it comes to taking them out again.

The import of all narcotics is strictly forbidden.

On leaving, there are a number of restrictions: exporting antiques is forbidden, and violation of this is treated very harshly; proof of purchase is required if you wish to take a new carpet out of the country, and to take an old carpet a certificate from a directorate of a museum is necessary. It is illegal to remove wild plants or animals. *See also* **Money**

Disabled Visitors

Facilities for disabled travellers are improving in İstanbul, although the steps and uneven pavements are intrinsic drawbacks. That said, the Turks are always willing to lend a helping hand if necessary. The airport has adapted lifts and toilets and the state theatres and concert halls have ramps. All the 5-star hotels have good facilities.

Long-haul Holidays and Travel is available from RADAR, 12 City Forum, 250 City Road, London EC1V 8AF, ☎ 0171 250 3222 between 10am and 4pm. It contains advice and information on transport, accommodation, equipment

and tour operators in many countries, including Turkey.

Driving

Visitors taking their own car to Turkey will require an international driving licence, the vehicle's registration document and a green card from your insurance company. You should ensure that your insurance covers you for accidents in Turkey. Travellers continuing to the Middle East will require a *Carnet de passage*. Visitors must exit the country with the same vehicle with which they entered. For stays exceeding six months, *see* **Before You Go**.

Traffic drives on the right in Turkey and the highway code is similar to that in Europe. Seat belts are compulsory in the front only. Speed limits are: **Motorways** 120kph/75mph **Main roads** 90kph/56mph **Built-up areas** 50kph/31mph

Petrol stations can easily be found all over the country and those on the main highway often have restaurants attached and are open around the clock.

It is not advisable to drive in İstanbul; it will save neither time nor money and take a heavy toll on your nerves.

Dry Cleaning *see* **Laundry**

Electric Current
The current is 220V all over Turkey.

Embassies *see* Consulates

Emergencies
The Tourist Police will usually be able to offer assistance in emergencies. They can be contacted at Beyoğlu ☎ (212) 253 7110 or at Eminonu ☎ (212) 522 2670. The main emergency services are:
Police ☎ 155
Traffic police ☎ 154
Gendarme ☎ 156
Fire service ☎ 110
Emergency ☎ 112

Etiquette
• In Turkey, you are regarded as a **konuk**, meaning a guest. You will be made to feel very welcome wherever you go and often offered tea, which would cause offence if refused.
• When entering a mosque, remove your shoes and leave them outside. Women should cover their hair with a scarf and refrain from wearing immodest clothing, such as shorts. Some mosques provide overskirts.
• Avoid visiting mosques on Fridays or prayer times (many large mosques close to non Muslims at midday for an hour).
• A traditionally Muslim but

also secular country, Turkey has no special legislation with regard to alcohol consumption. However, it is appreciated if you do not drink alcohol during Ramadan, especially in the small villages.
• Any public display of affection between a man and a woman is considered offensive.
• Avoid pointing a finger.
• Women should dress modestly and avoid direct eye contact with men, as this can be taken as a sign of encouragement.
• Women walking alone or in pairs late at night can expect unwelcome attention.
• Nodding the head means 'no' and shaking the head means 'yes'.
• Some Turks do not like to be photographed, so ask their permission first, and do not be surprised if they expect payment, as this is common practice in Turkey.

Excursions
A boat trip around the Bosphorus strait is a must while staying in İstanbul. The round trip takes about six hours and is reasonably priced. Many companies offer commentaries in English and other languages, and a night trip is always an option (*see* Princes' Islands p.84).

Slicing meat for kebabs.

Travel agents arrange numerous other tours, both around the city's sights and further afield, all of which have professional guides who speak English. Hotels also have information about organised excursions. Those wishing to organise their own trips can obtain a guide from the Ministry of Tourism offices.

Guidebooks *see* Maps

Health

Any medical treatment by a doctor or hospital has to be paid for in Turkey, so adequate medical insurance taken out at home is essential.

There are no particular health risks in İstanbul, but beware of uncooked food and drink only bottled water as a precaution against stomach upsets. Diarrhoea is a common problem, sometimes caused by bad food but often just by the change in diet and water. A day or so in bed, with plenty of water, rehydrating powder (e.g. diarrorlyte) and bland food should sort it out. Guard, too, against the sun.

For any minor ailments visit a pharmacy (*eczane*), as Turkish pharmacists are highly qualified and may speak English (main chemists only); most drugs can be bought over the counter without a prescription. At least one pharmacy is open 24 hours a day in the city, the location of which is posted in the other pharmacies.

If a doctor is required, your hotel will call one for you but a charge will be made. If hospital treatment is needed, it is best to go to one of the foreign hospitals in İstanbul:
American Hospital, Güzelbahçe Sokak 20, Nişantaşı ☎ (212) 231 4050
International Hospital, İstanbul Caddesi, Yeşilköy ☎ (212) 663 3000.

Hours *see* Opening Hours

Hello Merhaba
Goodbye Allahaısmarladık (said by the person leaving)
            Güle güle (said by the person staying)
or   İyi günler (good day) or iyi geceler (good night)
Please Lütfen
Thank you Teşekkür ederim or mersi
Thanks Teşekkürler
Yes Evet
No Hayır
I want İstiyorum
How much is this? Bu ne kadar?
When? Ne zaman?
Where is it? Nerede?
What is the time? Saat kaç
Beer Bira
Wine Şarap
Water Su
Mineral water Maden suyu
Tea Çay
Coffee Kahve
The bill Hesap
Large/small Büyük/Küçük

Information see **Tourist Information Offices**

Language
English is reasonably widely spoken, but there are many times when someone serving you will not understand English. That said, a kind customer will often come to the rescue. Turkish, written in the Latin alphabet, belongs to the Ural-Altaic group of languages and has an affinity with Finnish and Hungarian; it is unrelated to European languages or Arabic.

Above are a few words to help you during your stay.

Laundry
There are no self-service launderettes in İstanbul, but 24-hour dry cleaners and laundries abound. All hotels offer a laundry service.

Maps
The *Michelin Green Guide Europe* has a section on Turkey, which

includes detailed information on the main attractions in İstanbul, together with maps of the city. The guide also contains information on attractions outside the city, and provides useful background information.

Michelin on the Net
www.michelin-travel.com.
This route-planning service covers all of Europe. Options which allow you to choose a route are updated three times weekly, integrating on-going road-works, etc. Descriptions include distances and travelling times between towns, selected hotels and restaurants.

Medical Care *see* Health

Money
The national monetary unit is the Turkish Lira (TL), with notes in denominations of 50 000, 100 000, 250 000, 500 000 and 1 000 000 lira, and coins in denominations of 5 000, 10 000 and 25 000 lira.

Eurocheques can be cashed at most banks, PTTs (*see* **Post Offices**) and larger hotels, as can travellers' cheques upon producing identification. Exchange offices, found at the main tourist sights and at border crossings, are open Saturdays and often on Sundays, and generally offer the best rates. The rate of inflation is very high (80 per cent over the last few years).

Banks are open from 8.30am-noon and 1.30-5pm, Monday to Friday, but cash dispensers are available outside these hours. The most widely accepted credit cards are Eurocard, Diner's Club, Visa and Mastercard.

There is no limit to the amount of foreign currency that may be taken into Turkey, but not more than $5 000 worth of Turkish currency may be taken into or out of the country. The exchange slips should be retained as you may be required to show them when converting Turkish lira back into foreign currency or when taking expensive souvenirs out of the country to prove they have been bought with legal currency.

It is possible to obtain a tax refund on some items when purchased from authorised outlets, identifiable by certificates or stickers on display. Ask the retailer concerned, about this.

Newspapers
Foreign newspapers and magazines are available in İstanbul and other large cities and tourist resorts one day

after publication, though they can be expensive.

The *Turkish Daily News,* the only English-language daily, is useful for events and what's going on. *Cornucopia* magazine contains useful information on Turkey.

Opening Hours

Generally, the **shops** in İstanbul are open from 9.30am-7pm. Some may close between 1pm and 2pm. In tourist areas closing times vary, with some shops staying open to about midnight. The Grand Bazaar in İstanbul is open from 8am-7pm and is closed on Sundays. On the first day of the religious holidays (Şeker Bayramı and Kurban Bayramı) all shops and bazaars are closed. These festivals follow the lunar calendar therefore take place 11 days before they occurred the previous year.

Most **museums** and **palaces** are open from 8.30am-noon and 1.30-5pm. The most usual closing day is Monday, although there are several exceptions, including the Topkapı Palace, which is closed on Tuesdays; some places close on a Sunday as well.

Government offices are open from 8.30am-12.30pm and 1.30-5.30pm. They are closed Saturdays and Sundays

except in tourist areas, where they are open daily. *See also* **Money** and **Post Offices**

Photography

International brands of film are readily available in İstanbul as is 24-hour processing.

If you want to take photographs or films inside a museum or at an ancient site, a fee must be paid, and always be on the look-out for (and obey) signs forbidding photography. Military areas and airports are particularly sensitive areas.

If you want to take photographs of people, ask permission first.

Police

There are three categories of police in Turkey. The Tourist Police are for the sole benefit of tourists and should be turned to for help in the event of any mishap. They have offices all over the country; in İstanbul they are based at Yerebatan Caddesi 6 ☎ (212) 528 5369. In an emergency ☎ 155.

Traffic police deal with motoring problems (☎ 154 in the event of a traffic accident).

The market police can be seen in the markets and bazaars, making sure no illegal practices are carried out.

In addition, the Gendarme,

soldiers in green army uniform, help prevent serious crimes such as smuggling and drug dealing.

Visitors should always carry their passport as a means of identification (this is a legal requirement).

Post Offices

Turkish post offices can be recognised by their yellow 'PTT' signs. The main branches are open from 8am-midnight from Monday to Saturday and from 9am-7pm on Sundays. Small post offices have the same hours as Government Offices (*see* **Opening Hours**).

Poste restante letters should be addressed 'postrestant' to the central post office (*Merkez Postanesi*). Proof of identity must be presented on collection.

Other PTT services include sending and receiving faxes, dispatching valuable documents, and exchanging money, travellers' cheques and international postal orders. Phone calls can also be made from PTTs (*see* **Telephones**).

Stamps can be bought from post offices, hotels, sweet and cigarette kiosks and some souvenir shops.

Religion

Turkey is a Moslem country and there are mosques in most streets throughout the country. In İstanbul, where there are sizeable Christian and Jewish communities, there are Anglican churches and synagogues, too.

Smoking

Smoking is widely tolerated in İstanbul, but local laws have recently been passed banning smoking in public places. Cigarettes are available from kiosks, newsagents and general stores.

Taxis *see* **Transport**

Telephones

The cheapest way to make a telephone call in Turkey is from a booth in a PTT (*see* **Post Offices**). Although most of the better hotels have direct-dial international lines from rooms, the cost will be considerably more. Phone cards and *jetons,* available in three sizes for local, inter-city and international calls, can be bought at all PTTs. Inter-city operator ☎ 131 Directory enquiries ☎ 118 The area code for İstanbul (Europe) is ☎ 212 and for İstanbul (Asia) ☎ 216 International country codes are as follows:

Australia: ☎ 00 61
Canada: ☎ 00 1
Ireland: ☎ 00 353
New Zealand: ☎ 00 64
UK: ☎ 00 44
USA: ☎ 00 1

Time Difference
Turkish time observes
Greenwich Mean Time (GMT)
plus two hours.

Tipping
In restaurants, if service is not
included in the bill, 10 per
cent is expected. Taxis do not
expect a tip.

Toilets
There are a number of public
toilets in İstanbul (they can also
usually be found in mosque
courtyards), although toilet
paper is not always provided
and they may be the hole-in-the
floor variety. You need to pay a
fee at most public toilets (often
posted outside the toilets).
Generally, plumbing and
hygiene is good. In luxury
hotels you can flush the paper
down the toilets, but in many
you will have to put it in the
bin provided. If there is an
attendant, a small tip is
expected.

Signs read WC; Men is
Bay/Baylara or *Erkeklere*;
Women is *Bayan/Bayanlara* or
Kadınlara.

Tourist Information Offices
Tourist offices in İstanbul can
be found at the Hilton Hotel,
Sultanahmet Square, Karaköy
Maritime Station, Sirkeci Tram
Station, plus the airport; the
central office is at Meşrutiyet
Caddesi 57/5 ☎ (212) 243 3472.

Turkish Information Offices
abroad:
Australia Suite 101, 280
George Street, Sydney NSW
2 000 ☎ 92 23 3055
Canada Constitution Square,
360 Albert Street, Suite 801,
Ottawa, Ontario K1R 7X7
☎ 230 8654
UK 170–173 Piccadilly,
London W1V 9DD
☎ 0171 629 7771
US 821 United Nations Plaza,
New York, NY 10017
☎ 429 9844

Tours see Excursions

Transport
The cheapest way of getting
about the city is in a *dolmuş*, a
public taxi that travels along
specified, fixed routes. You pay
a set fare according to the
distance travelled and can flag
them down anywhere – they
indicate their route on the roof
or by the side doors.

Ordinary yellow taxis, are
metered; fares increase after
midnight. Check that the
meter is on at the start of the

journey, and that it is set on the correct rate: day/ *Gun* or night/ *Gece*.

High-speed trams operate in the city between İkitelli, Aksaray and Sirkeci, while the old tramway operates in the Beyoğlu district between Taksim and Tünel.

Public buses within the city tend to be crowded and rather slow and a ticket (or *carnet*, a book of tickets) must be bought in advance from special kiosks.

The ferry boat is a practical and enjoyable means of transport and there are several departures from Eminönü to various parts of the city.

If you are travelling out of İstanbul, there is a choice of public transport. Turkish State Railways connect most major cities and a offer a choice of first- and second-class seating. Most trains have sleeping cars and restaurants. There are two train stations: Sirkeci on the European side, and Haydarpaşa on the Asian side.

Alternatively, independent coach companies provide comfortable, air-conditioned buses to most major cities day and night from the bus terminal at Esenler. This service is efficient and relatively inexpensive; book at bus stations or travel agents.

For long hauls, THY operates several internal flights to most large cities across the country (*see* **Getting There**).

TV and Radio

There are both state and private TV channels, both broadcasting in Turkish. The larger hotels will offer cable or satellite TV, possibly with CNN, NBC, Euronews and Eurosport, and BBC Prime – all in English or other European languages. Tourism Radio, on 101.6MHZ (in İstanbul), broadcasts the news in English, French and German from 8.30-10.30am, 12.30-6.30pm and at 9.30pm. Feature programmes are also broadcast in these languages.

Water

Tap water, now chlorinated, is reckoned to be safe to drink in İstanbul but nevertheless it is probably best to stick to bottled water which is readily available.

INDEX

INDEX